# Introduction

The first six walks in this book a[re from] Harlech – the Bron y Graig Uchaf [car park next] to a bus stop. Its location is shown on the map opposite. Care is needed not to confuse it with the nearby Bron y Graig Isaf (lower) short-stay car park. **The remaining nine walks** are located close to Harlech, with none of their starting points more than a 20 minute drive from the town.

The location of all the walks is indicated on the back cover map, and a summary of the key features and length of all the walks is given in the chart on the inside back cover. The walks vary in length between 2½ miles and 6 miles. All can be managed by a reasonably fit person, but in this area there are, of course, some uphill sections.

The name 'Harlech' is thought to be derived from the term 'beautiful slope'. Walks **2** to **6** take you up the 'slope' to enjoy the outstanding views over a wide sea and an even bigger sky. Sunsets, if you can arrange to be out to see one, will be long remembered. And once on the crest of the 'slope' there are also extensive views in the other directions far to the north and east. Many of the high mountains of the Snowdonia National Park can be seen.

Walks **7** to **15** take you to areas a little further into the countryside around Harlech. The evidence provided by the many standing stones, burial places, homesteads and hut circles makes it certain that the area was first settled many thousands of years ago. And from relatively more recent times there are remains of hillforts and trackways. It is a rich source for anyone interested in ancient history.

For the general countryside lover too the area is exceptional. It is attention-holding landscape. There are so many wonderful rock out-croppings. Oak trees can appear to grow out of the rock faces, and woodland floors have boulders covered with thick green cushions of moss. Mosses are on stone walls and even up tree trunks, sometimes with ferns high up which wave to you in the gentlest of breezes.

Most surprisingly, there are places where you can stand and look around, and imagine yourself to be in any time period since the glaciers retreated, because there is no evidence of what man has done since. It is special. Go slowly and quietly, and these walks will give you a taste of this precious area. Maybe you will want to explore it further.

## WALK I
# HARLECH BEACH via THE DUNES

**DESCRIPTION** This easy 2½ mile walk takes a not-so-well known route through the town's outskirts, has the classic view of the Castle, and uses a sandy path across the dunes to reach a section of the beach much less used than that reached from the popular beach car park.

**START** The Bron y Graig Uchaf long-stay car park (not to be confused with the Bron y Graig Isaf short-stay car park). See the map on the inside front cover.

**1** From the car park go out onto the road. Turn RIGHT along it and go down to the main road and shops. Turn LEFT along the main road and go past the shops. Where the pavement on the right hand side ends, take the signed footpath off to the RIGHT. Go up on to the rocky outcrops on the right to see the view indicator. *This is the place for the classic photographs of the Castle with some of the high Snowdonia mountains in the background.* Go back down to the path and turn RIGHT. Carry on down this path to reach the main (A496) road. Cross it carefully, and at a gap in the railing, go down seven steps and turn RIGHT along a narrow passageway. At the bottom turn LEFT, along a surfaced track. *The mixture of buildings now seen on your left is Coleg Harlech. This is an adult education college which opened in 1927. At its centre is the former house, Wern Fawr, built in 1908 by George Davison, then Managing Director in the U.K. of Kodak. Later, following the purchase of a villa in France, he was persuaded to sell it in 1925 to Cardiff businessman, Henry Gethin Lewis, who donated the property for use as a college for adult students. Created by a few determined people who could see the deficiencies in the formal education system, the college's history makes interesting reading.*

**2** After about 200 yards, go RIGHT through a waymarked gate and across the railway. Then take the waymarked path LEFT along a rough surfaced track. After about 200 yards, where the track curves left, take the clear wide path off to the right, heading more directly to the high dunes and the sea. Follow along this main sandy path. *There are fine views of the Castle behind to the right and opportunities to enjoy the dune flowers.* Go up over the high dunes, and the sea and beach come into view. Explore the beach, of course, but the route of this walk is to turn RIGHT (north) along it. *There are excellent views of some of the Snowdonia mountains from this part of the beach, and, of course, the Lleyn Peninsula.* Go along the beach for about ¾ mile, when the main entrance and exit is reached. It is at a wide gap in a fence safeguarding the dunes, and where there is a high red and white pole. Take the wide sandy track between wire fences. It later becomes surfaced and then joins a metalled road at the beach car park.

**3** Continue straight ahead towards the Castle. At the end of this road turn RIGHT, and just past the telephone box, go through the gate on the right and follow the path parallel to the road. After about 200 yards, where it is joined from the right by a path from the swimming pool, go LEFT across the railway and out on to the main road opposite a letter box. Cross the main road and go up the minor road signed 'Town Centre'. This zig-zags uphill (*there are seats!*) and where the road divides, go LEFT, past the 20% sign. When Harlech's main street is reached, go RIGHT to go back to the car park. There is a pleasant path to the car park off to the LEFT just before the Church entrance. *Look for the rock cannon holes (used in the celebration of important events with gunpowder) as you approach the car park.*

# WALK 1

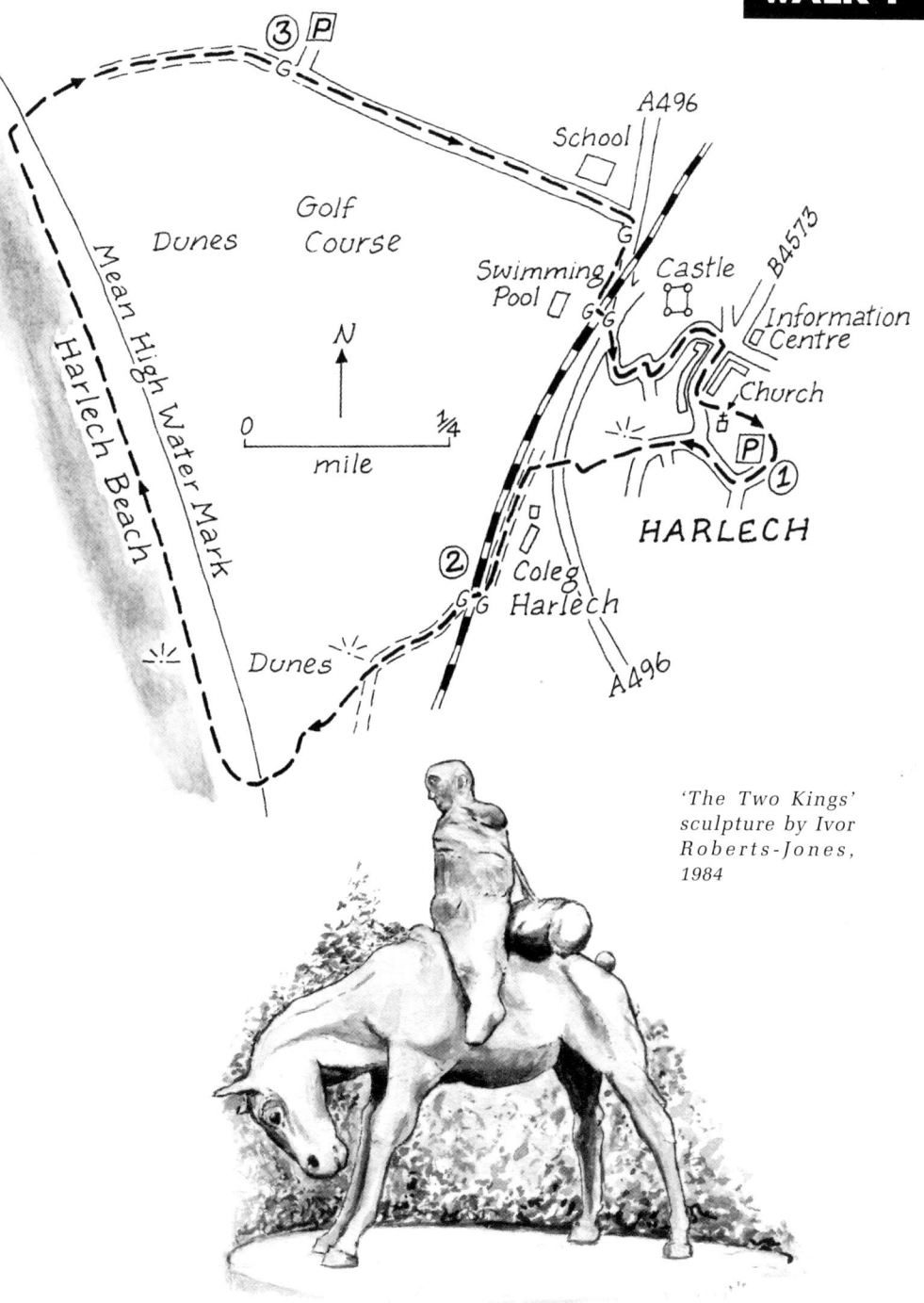

'The Two Kings' sculpture by Ivor Roberts-Jones, 1984

## WALK 2
# RHINOG VIEW

**DESCRIPTION** A 2½ mile walk going just over the 'slope' behind Harlech to give fine extensive views of the Rhinog range of mountains, not visible from the town. It passes former farmhouses and barns, and although uphill near the start, the final mile is all downhill with outstanding views along that whole length.
**START** The Bron y Graig Uchaf long-stay car park (not to be confused with the Bron y Graig Isaf short-stay car park). See the map on the inside front cover.

**1** From the car park go out onto the road and turn LEFT. Walk along to the end of the high stone wall on the right. Just beyond the gate to view the duck pond take a narrow path off RIGHT alongside the first house (no. 4). When it reaches a road, go RIGHT, and then almost immediately LEFT along another road. Go past a cemetery and keep on ahead along the rough surfaced track. Stay on this track until after passing, on the left, gates to the property Llys Bach. Then take the waymarked path slightly LEFT. This path later emerges at a surfaced road area. Carry on straight ahead along a path towards a small gate. Go through and ahead to another small gate and then on to a junction of signed paths.

**2** Take the path back sharp RIGHT, up into the trees and which follows close to a wall on the right. When the path comes out into the open, leave the wall and zig-zag half-LEFT up the field. *This is steep, but pausing gives a chance to enjoy the fine views.* Towards the top of the field pass along close to the high gorse and natural rock wall on the left and alongside a small sycamore tree. A waymark post on the wall ahead comes into view. Cross the wall at the post and go ahead as indicated up to a yellow-top-post at a grass track. Go LEFT along it up to a waymark and on to double gates in front of two houses. Go through and ahead along a waymarked walled track between the houses. Stay on this green lane until it ends at an old barn. Pass to the left of the barn over a stile. Carry on up the field (parallel to the long side wall of the barn) and through a gap in the wall ahead. Turn LEFT and through another wall gap. Now go RIGHT, up the field to a swing gate.

**3** Go through and LEFT and almost immediately, where the track divides, bear RIGHT up to a gate Garth Mawr. Go through the gate and stay on the track to reach the house. At the gate to the right of the house, go through and then sharp LEFT to go over a low stile in the wall. Go ahead across the field and over a waymarked gated stile in the wall and bushes. Carry on ahead at first, but then work half-RIGHT over to a curving wall. Follow this around with the wall on your left. Near the top of the field, go RIGHT to another gated stile. Go over and ahead, passing to the LEFT of an old building. Keeping ahead in the same direction, cross another stile in the wall ahead. Follow the path ahead through the gorse, across a bridged small stream and out over a stile onto a road. *Here there are fine views across to the Rhinog mountains. They reach about 2,500 feet and provide some fine ridge walking. Elsewhere on these mountains, and if away from the used paths, walking can sometimes be difficult, but nevertheless very rewarding in the enjoyment of the wild beauty and archaeological remains from prehistory to 19th century manganese workings. If you are tempted to get closer to them other walks in the book will take you nearer: Walk **9** is close to Moel Ysgyfarnogod in the north; Walks **14** and **15**, further south, give fine closer views of the three highest tops.*

**4** Go RIGHT along the road, staying on it for about ¼ mile to reach the next footpath sign at a gate on your right. Go through and ahead close to the wall on the right. When the wall veers right, go half-LEFT uphill to cross the wall ahead by the waymarked stile. Carry on ahead in the same direction and, at the crest, aim for the ladder stile now in view in the wall ahead. *There is a strangely positioned, and no doubt now redundant, trig point in this field, to the right over by the wall. The OS map shows it at a*

# WALK 2

Garth Mawr

height of 258 metres, but it is not at the highest point. Anyway, there are fine views from here, and it is certainly worth pausing. Cross the ladder stile and drop straight down to a swing gate. Go through into the walled lane and down over a stile to pass to the left of the house Groes Lwyd. A minor road starts here and can be followed ¾ mile downhill all the way to Harlech, turning right at the T junction

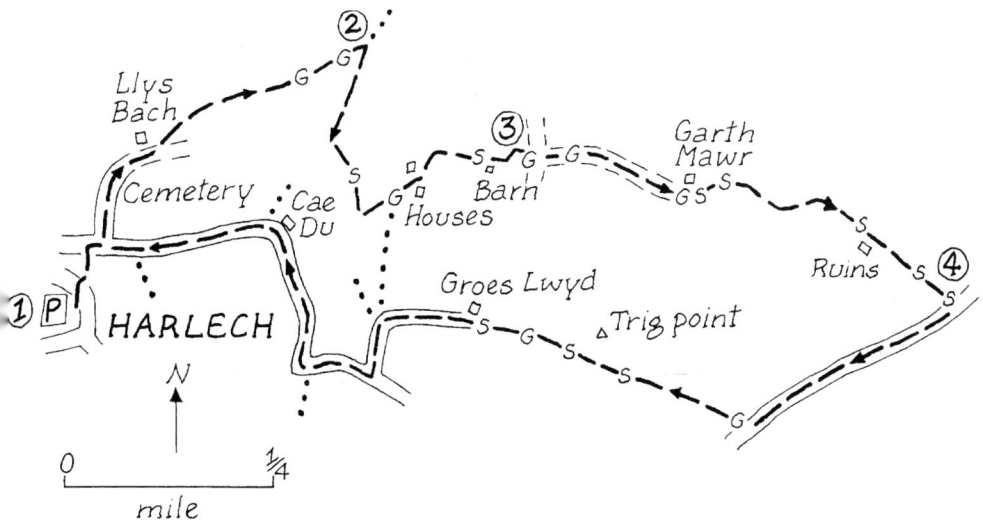

## WALK 3
# FOEL SENIGL

**DESCRIPTION** This 4 mile walk goes to the top of Foel Senigl, the nearest of the hills behind Harlech. Although only 1000 feet high, its detached position gives wonderful all-round distant views and it is well worth the moderate ascent. As with other walks, the views all along the route will make you want to go slowly.
**START** The Bron y Graig Uchaf long-stay car park (not to be confused with the Bron y Graig Isaf short-stay car park). See the map on the inside front cover.

**1** From the car park go out onto the road and turn LEFT. Walk along to the end of the high stone wall on the right. Just beyond the gate to view the duck pond, take a narrow path off RIGHT alongside the first house (no. 4). When it reaches a road, go RIGHT. *After about 100 yards there is an old Scotch Baptist Chapel baptism pool, created in 1841.* Carry on along the road, past the house Cae Du and up past an old barn on the right *(a listed building, with graded slate roof and built, like many in this area, into the hillside slope, usually to give easy access at the back to an upper storage area).* Just beyond the barn take an unsigned path LEFT at a gap between two walls, and which soon reaches a swing gate.

**2** Go through and carry on ahead along a fairly wide track which climbs gradually up the slope of this field. Further along it curves right and reaches double gates in front of two houses. Go through and ahead along a waymarked track between the houses. Stay on this green lane until it ends at an old barn. Pass to the left of the barn over a stile. Carry on up the field (parallel to the long side wall of the barn) and through a gap in the wall ahead. Turn LEFT and through another wall gap. Carry on ahead, close to the wall on the left, to go over the most substantial historic wall crossing in the area. **Ignore** the wall gap now on the left and carry on ahead alongside the wall on the left. Pass to the left of the house which soon appears ahead and reach a waymark at a gate on the right. Go through and up to another waymark at a metal gate in sight ahead. Go through this gate and LEFT across the field to a stile in the fence.

**3** Cross the stile and walk up some steps to another waymarked stile in the wall on the left. Go over, then partly LEFT over some exposed surface rock. Then aim to go across the field passing to the right of some piled field clearance stones and on to a slightly raised path to a swing gate in the wall ahead. Go through and ahead alongside a low wall on the left. Cross the waymarked stile at the next wall and go through a small gate in the wall up ahead. Go ahead with a high wall on the left, but soon go half-RIGHT up to another similar small gate in the next wall. Pass through and then half-RIGHT ahead, passing to the right of a small mound and towards an isolated hawthorn bush. Go past and on ahead in the same direction towards the roof of the house Hendre-ddyfrgl which is now in sight. Keep on this line and pass left of the waymark ahead and go down a faint track, still towards the house. When this track reaches another wider track at the wall below, go LEFT and then shortly RIGHT through a metal gate.

**4** Go across the field and up through a small gate in the wall beyond Hendre. Keep ahead in the same direction and go through a wooden gate in the next wall. Carry on through the next gate ahead and along the track to the farm Merthyr. Pass to the LEFT of the farmhouse and turn RIGHT immediately behind it, up along a rough sur-

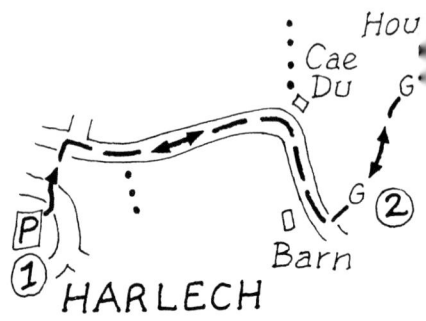

# WALK 3

faced wide track. This track leaves the farm area through a gate where a stone wall starts on the left. About 50 yards after this gate, and in an open area, go 90 degrees RIGHT, and pass to the right of a small mound. At the crest of the field slope, aim for the gate ahead between a fence and a stone wall. Go through, carrying on in the same direction, and reach a small metal gate in the wall ahead. It is just to the right of the old stone step-stile crossing, which you may prefer to use.

**5** When through the wall, go LEFT uphill to the top. *Take advantage of the sturdy double-sided bench erected in 2002 in memory of Don Murphy who lived nearby and who loved the views here. At just over 1000 feet, Foel Senigl is the highest point on any of the six walks starting in Harlech and gives exceptional all around views. Snowdon to the north is 15 miles away, and the top of Bardsey Island, seen over the Lleyn Peninsula to the west, is twice that distance.* When you leave, carry on down the other side in roughly the same direction (southwards) finding the best way between the rock outcrops, and aiming for the high wall below. Near the wall, work RIGHT to reach a rough surfaced vehicle track.

Turn LEFT along it and follow it down and out on to the road. Turn RIGHT along the road but in about 75 yards, go RIGHT over a stile and diagonally across the field, over a bridged small stream, and on through the gorse to a waymarked step-stile over the wall ahead.

**6** Cross and carry on ahead approaching a stone wall with a fence on top. Do NOT go through the gate ahead but keep RIGHT, going along the wall and passing to the right of a ruined building. Just beyond the building, cross the wall through a small gated step-stile and carry on ahead. As another stone wall is approached, go LEFT and downhill. Follow close to the wall as it curves RIGHT, but when the wall curves right again keep on straight ahead towards an isolated large standing rock. About 20 yards before reaching this rock, go sharp LEFT towards the bushes and a wall. Find the gated stile over it at a waymark post, and cross. Continue up to the house Garth Mawr and cross the low stile in the low wall to the left of the house. Turn RIGHT and go through the gate onto the vehicle track leading **up the slope** from the house. Continue along this track, later going through a gate. Shortly after this gate, and where another track joins it from the right, go RIGHT through a swing gate and down to the barn passed on the outward walk. Carry on along the lane to go between the houses, through the double gate, and down the path to the road back to Harlech.

## WALK 4
# MURIAU GWYDDELOD
## (Irishmen's Walls)

**DESCRIPTION** This 2½ mile walk takes you up on the slopes behind Harlech for fine views, firstly over the beach to the Lleyn Peninsula and to the mountains of northern Snowdonia, and then later to the extensive range of the Rhinog mountains 5 miles east of Harlech. It passes, and you can visit, an important ancient hut settlement.

**START** The Bron y Graig Uchaf long-stay car park (not to be confused with the Bron y Graig Isaf short-stay car park). See the map on the inside front cover.

**1** From the car park go out on to the road and turn LEFT. Walk along to the end of the high stone wall on the right. Just beyond the gate where you can view the duck pond, take a narrow path off RIGHT alongside the first house (no. 4). When it reaches a road, go RIGHT. *In about 100 yards there is a Scotch Baptist Chapel baptism pool created in 1841.* Carry on along the road, past the house Cae Du and up past an old barn on the right (*a listed building with graded slate roof and built, like many in this area, into the hillside slope often to give easy access at the back to an upper storage area*). Further along, the road turns sharp left. A few yards after this bend, go RIGHT, through a gate along a signed footpath. *From about here there are the first fine views back over the beach to Criccieth and the Lleyn Peninsula, the Glaslyn and Dwyryd estuaries, Portmeirion, and the high mountains of Snowdonia beyond.*

**2** On reaching the farmhouse Cefnfilltir, follow the waymark direction LEFT towards the barns, then RIGHT through a waymarked gate and on ahead to go to the right of the barn facing you. Go through another gate, turn LEFT to reach another waymark and RIGHT through the gate as indicated. Keep ahead along the wide walled track until it ends in an open field. Go LEFT up alongside a wall, over a small stream and through a wide gap in an old wall slightly RIGHT ahead. Cross the same stream again ahead and go up through a gap in a substantial wall. At the open hillside take a route roughly diagonally across the field. As the crest of the hill top is being approached, aim for a large triangular shaped standing rock and, beyond it, a waymarked post. At the post, go LEFT to a fence-topped wall with a waymarked stile over it. *The extensive new views now ahead are to the east and the Rhinog mountains.* Cross the stile and the next one just 30 yards further ahead on to the road.

**3** Turn RIGHT along it. After about 300 yards go over the signed ladder stile on the right. *In this field, just to the right (and marked on the 1:25,000 OS map) are two ancient hut groups known as Muriau Gwyddelod (or the Irishmen's Walls) with well-preserved foundations. They are interpreted as courtyard houses – circular huts within an enclosed yard, and called Enclosed Homesteads, thought to be occupied through pre-Roman and Roman times. They are part of much of pre-historic interest in this area of ancient landscape.* To continue the walk, aim diagonally (south-west) across the field in the general direction indicated by the sign at the ladder stile, to the western corner of the field where two walls meet. In the corner, cross the stone step-stile and go ahead alongside an old wall on the left. At the next corner go LEFT through a gap and then immediately very sharp back RIGHT to go along a walled grass lane ahead. After about 100 yards go through the gap on the right and then immediately LEFT along the wall to another gap ahead. From this gap go half-RIGHT across to a waymarked post and over a stone stile.

**4** Go half-RIGHT across the next field, skirting to the right of a depression, and aim for a gap in the low wall ahead. Pass through and half-LEFT down to a low post waymark and on to reach a waymarked gate in the bottom corner. Go through and RIGHT

# WALK 4

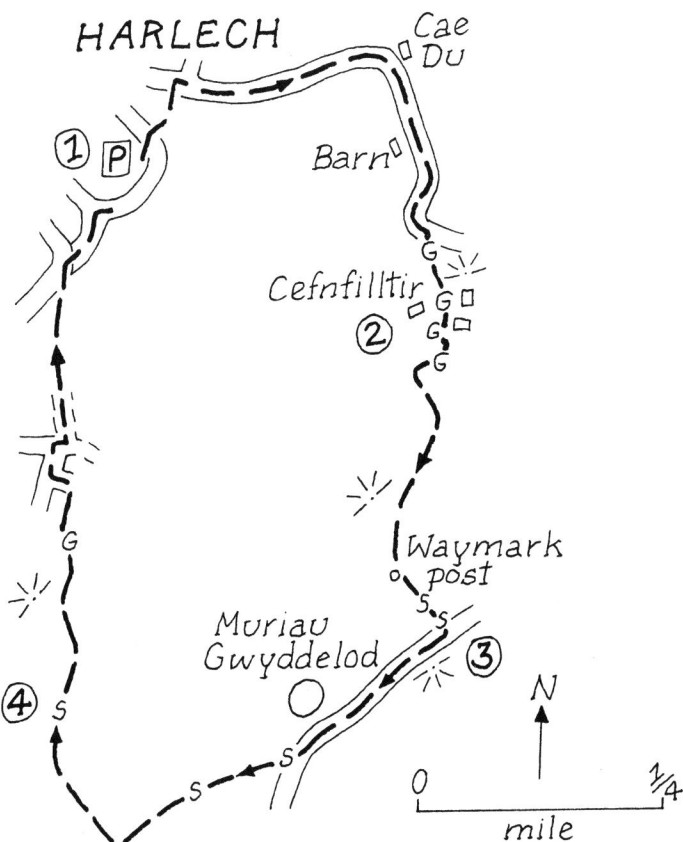

along a grass track to reach a road. Go ahead and RIGHT around three sides of a high wall. At the end of the final side, as a field gate is approached, go LEFT down a rough surfaced track past a domestic garage on the left, and into a shady lane. When this lane reaches a road go RIGHT. Where, very shortly, the road bends left for vehicles, keep on ahead and down to reach the car park.

## About the author, Geoff Elliott

**G**eoff has strong feelings for the landscape of the old county of Meirionnydd. Always a very keen walker, he has known the area for 50 years. Born in Cardiff, and spending his working life there, he moved on early retirement to Dolgellau (where he wrote his book **Local Walks Around Dolgellau** in this series) and later to Harlech. He considers the area of these walks to be special, and wrote the book to help others discover and enjoy the attractions it holds. He is an active member of the Ramblers' Association and a voluntary Snowdonia National Park warden.

## WALK 5
# HISTORIC STILES

**DESCRIPTION** A 4 mile walk into an area of quiet and beautiful countryside which few visitors see. On the way, and back, there are superb views and a chance to use interesting stiles left from another era.

**START** The Bron y Graig Uchaf long-stay car park (not to be confused with the Bron y Graig Isaf short-stay car park). See the map on the inside front cover.

**1** From the car park go out onto the road. Turn LEFT, and in 20 yards take the track RIGHT up steps into a local nature reserve. *This area was originally part of the estate of a now demolished large house, Bron y Graig, and was acquired by the local authority in 1972.* Follow this path around to the right. After about ¼ mile it bends right and drops down towards a caravan site. At the bottom take the narrow path LEFT, with the caravans on the right. This path emerges at a rough surfaced lane. Go LEFT, then almost immediately RIGHT, following the high wall on your left. At the surfaced road go LEFT, keeping to the wall, and shortly LEFT again to reach a waymarked post. Go RIGHT, as indicated, along a grassy track to reach three gates. Go through the first gate immediately on the left and uphill with a wall on the right. Pass through the gap in the wall ahead and carry on uphill. When the wall on the right curves right, keep straight on to reach a stone step-stile in the wall ahead. Cross and carry on straight ahead uphill. *There are fine views back across the bay.* Near the top, go through a gap in the wall and then aim slightly LEFT for a waymarked post on the horizon. At the post carry on slightly RIGHT to another post on top of the stone wall ahead. Go over the stile and ahead to the next one. *There are now extensive views ahead to the rounded hill, Moelfre, and behind it and to the left, the mountains of the Rhinog range.*

**2** Cross the road and go over the stile opposite. Take a route roughly half-LEFT to reach, in about 150 yards, a faint farm vehicle track. Turn RIGHT along it through a gap towards a barn. When at the barn, follow the track LEFT through a gate and keep on it to reach a wall. Stay on the track as it goes to the right alongside the wall. *There are now more extensive views ahead to the Rhinog mountains and to the coast well beyond Barmouth.* At the field corner keep on the track, now walled on both sides, to reach some barns. Pass to the right of the barns, through a gate and on ahead as waymarked. On approaching a line of trees ahead, curve around LEFT and through another gate. Follow the track down curving right, and then out through a gate to the farm Tyddyn-du and a road. Go RIGHT, along the road for about ¼ mile to reach a double footpath sign.

**3** Turn RIGHT here along the path up and over the rising ground then down, curving right, past high gorse and some oak trees, to reach laid stepping stones ahead approaching a wall. Go over the step-stile and carry on ahead uphill through the gorse. In the slightly clearer area, continue uphill but near the top veer LEFT to a wall and a waymarked post. Go through and RIGHT, as indicated, up to another waymark, then sharp LEFT along a wall. Continue LEFT to go past the house and then at a rough surfaced vehicle track go LEFT along it. After about ¼ mile, near the top of a rise, a metal gate is reached. *From a nearby wooden gate a little higher up and 20 yards to the right (north) the outer circular wall of an ancient homestead can be seen. It is marked on the OS 1:25,000 map.* Go through the **metal** gate and along the track to reach a surfaced road. Go RIGHT over the cattle grid and along to reach another cattle grid at a road junction.

**4** Turn RIGHT here and go ½ mile along this road. 100 yards after the road enters a long straight (*with fine views again east to the Rhinogs*) go LEFT at a double-signed stile (recognise it?) and then over the one in the wall 30 yards ahead. Continue ahead to the waymarked post. At it, go half-LEFT down and through a gap in the wall, then half-RIGHT down to the corner of the field.

10

# WALK 5

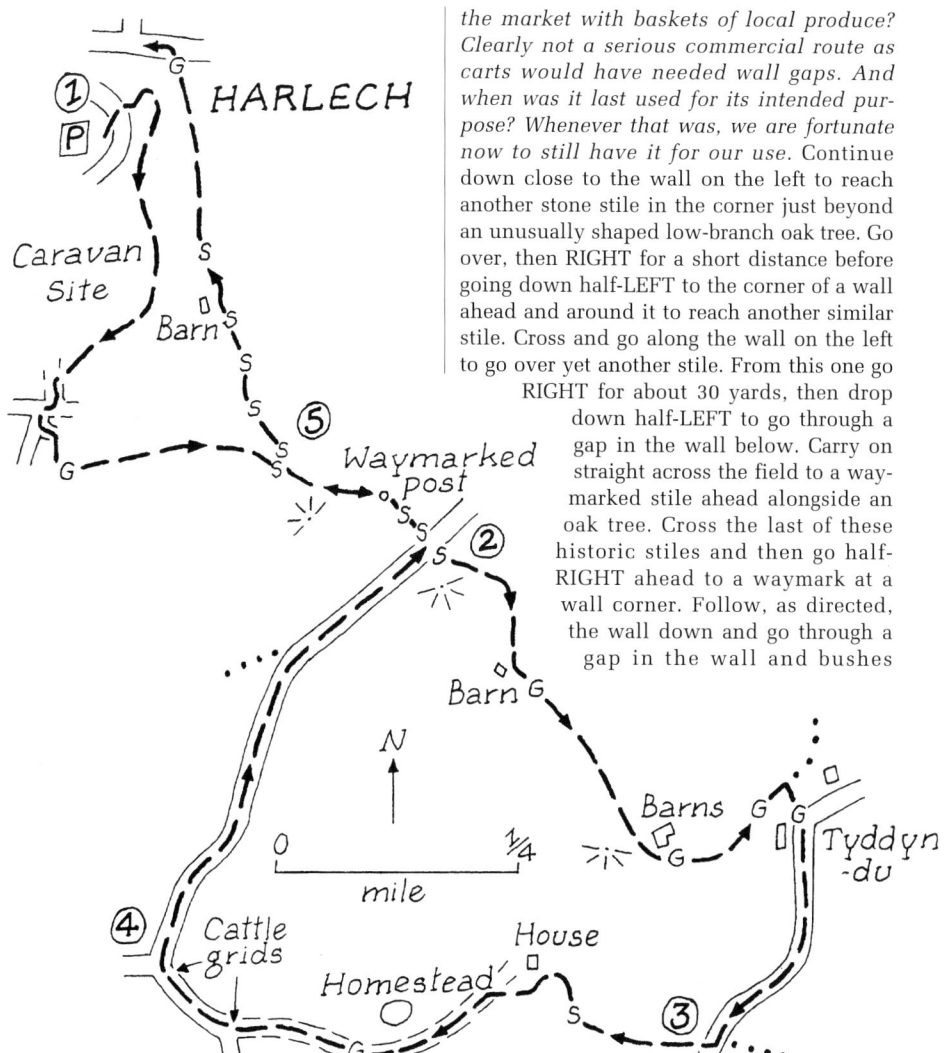

the market with baskets of local produce? Clearly not a serious commercial route as carts would have needed wall gaps. And when was it last used for its intended purpose? Whenever that was, we are fortunate now to still have it for our use. Continue down close to the wall on the left to reach another stone stile in the corner just beyond an unusually shaped low-branch oak tree. Go over, then RIGHT for a short distance before going down half-LEFT to the corner of a wall ahead and around it to reach another similar stile. Cross and go along the wall on the left to go over yet another stile. From this one go RIGHT for about 30 yards, then drop down half-LEFT to go through a gap in the wall below. Carry on straight across the field to a waymarked stile ahead alongside an oak tree. Cross the last of these historic stiles and then go half-RIGHT ahead to a waymark at a wall corner. Follow, as directed, the wall down and go through a gap in the wall and bushes

**5** Care is needed as the walls are approached as there are two stone stepstiles over them. Go over the one to the right. This is the start of a number of these historic stiles, close together and constructed so carefully and substantially into the field walls. They were probably built about 200 years ago and this must have been a well-used route. To the chapels perhaps, to school, to

ahead. Keep on ahead down to the next wall, then LEFT through a gap, and in 20 yards go RIGHT through another gap. Turn LEFT and follow the rough track down to reach a road. Go LEFT along the road. Stay on it to reach Harlech's main street or, to return directly to the car park, go off it LEFT through a gap in the wall just before the 20% sign.

11

## WALK 6
# HARLECH BEACH
## via
# LLANFAIR CLIFF

**DESCRIPTION** This 4 mile walk, including just over 1 mile along the beach, first goes across the open countryside behind Harlech giving outstanding views over Tremadog Bay. It then goes through part of Harlech's quiet neighbouring village Llanfair, and to the top of high cliffs for the unexpected and stunning view of the whole length of the beach. The route then follows the fine zig-zag path directly down.

**START** The Bron y Graig Uchaf long-stay car park (not to be confused with the Bron y Graig Isaf short-stay car park). See the map on the inside front cover.

**1** From the car park go out onto the road. Turn RIGHT along it and at the first T-junction go LEFT uphill. Where that road meets another coming up from the right, go LEFT along the road for 50 yards and take the signed path half-LEFT. When it meets a rough surfaced track at a high wall go RIGHT as waymarked. At the surfaced road go LEFT keeping to the wall, and in 30 yards, LEFT again to a waymarked post. Go RIGHT, as indicated, along the grass track. When three gates are reached, go through the recessed middle one and on half-RIGHT up the field to reach a low waymark post. Carry on as indicated, and through a gap in a low wall. Continue ahead, going very slightly LEFT, still rising and just skirting to the left of a natural depression. *It is worth pausing about here to look right and back for the extensive views. The Moelwyns on the extreme right (north), Snowdon (15 miles away) a little to the left and then the whole sweep of the Lleyn Peninsula with the top of Bardsey Island (30 miles away) just visible over the last section of land.* Keep ahead in the same direction and go over a waymarked stile in the wall.

**2** Continue half-RIGHT up to another wall and the field corner. Go LEFT through the gap and follow the wall on the right. At the next field corner go RIGHT, through the gap and then LEFT along the green lane. When this lane ends at an open field, turn RIGHT and follow the stone wall. Keep straight ahead where the wall has a kink to the right, and ignore the wall gap. Continue on down to a waymarked stone stile. Do NOT cross it but go LEFT along the wall. At the end go out through a small gate onto the road and go RIGHT. Where the road bends right, go LEFT over the cattle grid and then take the grass track half-RIGHT. When this reaches a metal gate, go through and half-RIGHT diagonally across the field, passing to the right of two large piles of field clearance stones. Near the field corner look for and go over the stone step-stile a little to the right. Carry on down ahead along the wall on the left. At this next field corner go through the gate ahead and carry on straight down to reach a green lane and go out on to a road. Turn RIGHT and reach a crossroads. *The chapel at this corner, Gaer Salem, was built in 1863.*

**3** Cross and continue down to another cross roads. Go RIGHT and continue along the pavement for just over 100 yards until at the entrance to the property Murmur-y-Don and directly opposite the signed entrance to the National Trust property Allt y Mor. Cross the road with care and go through a gate. *It is then certainly worth using the nearby seat to enjoy the best possible view of Harlech beach: almost 4 miles of unspoilt dune-backed coast and with the mountains of northern Snowdonia far beyond.* When ready, go down the zig-zag path to cross the railway and onto the beach. Go along it to the RIGHT (north) to reach the main exit at a wide gap in a fence safeguarding the dunes and where there is a high red and white pole. This sandy track soon becomes surfaced and joins a metalled road.

**4** Continue straight ahead towards the Castle. At the end of this road turn RIGHT, and just past the telephone box go through the gate on the right and follow the

# WALK 6

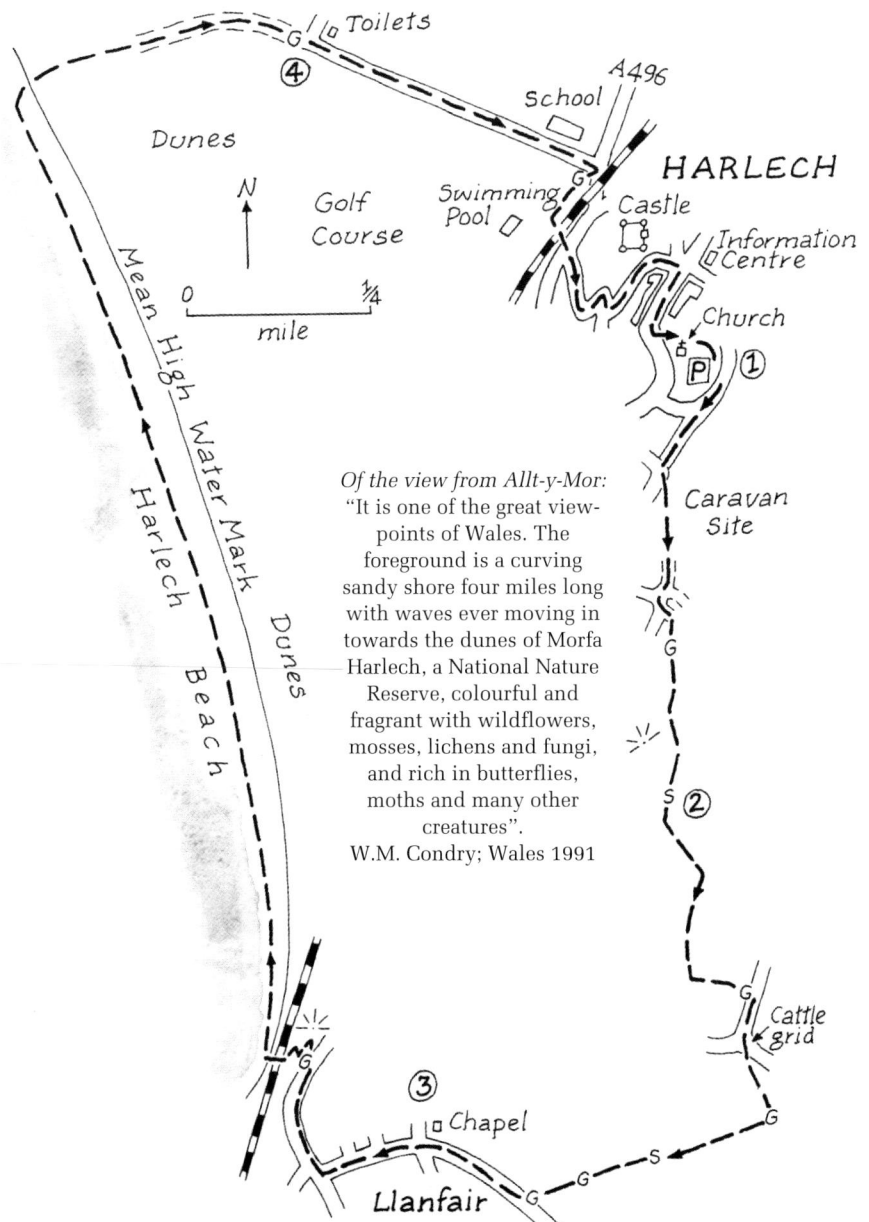

*Of the view from Allt-y-Mor:*
"It is one of the great viewpoints of Wales. The foreground is a curving sandy shore four miles long with waves ever moving in towards the dunes of Morfa Harlech, a National Nature Reserve, colourful and fragrant with wildflowers, mosses, lichens and fungi, and rich in butterflies, moths and many other creatures".
W.M. Condry; Wales 1991

path to the left. After about 200 yards, where it is joined on the right by a path from the swimming pool, go LEFT to cross the railway and the main road. Go up the minor road signed 'Town Centre'. This zig-zags uphill (*there are seats!*) and where the road divides, go LEFT, past the 20% sign. When Harlech's main street is reached go RIGHT. There is a pleasant path to the car park off to the LEFT just before the Church.

13

## WALK 7
# YNYS

**DESCRIPTION** An easy 3½ mile walk giving a chance to experience an area very different from those in the other walks. There are pleasant fields from which there are fine views, an interesting church yard and a section along an estuary, part of a National Nature Reserve, where you will want to take plenty of time. Take binoculars, if you can, for the estuary birdlife. Care needs to be taken about the tide. The ½ mile section along the estuary would occasionally not be possible at some high tides, and **do not** attempt it if high tide is approaching. A board, usually on the road at the side of the old warehouse at Ynys, gives the high tide time.

**START** At Glan-y-wern, using a layby just beyond the hamlet, along the east side of the A496 at GR 606249.

**DIRECTIONS** Go north from Harlech along the B4573 (or the A496 if more convenient). After nearly 4 miles, at the junction of the 'A' and 'B' roads at Glan-y-wern, park in the layby just beyond (north) of the road junction (NOT, please, the layby with the telephone box in front of the houses).

**1** From the layby, cross the road and go LEFT along it to the junction corner. DO NOT cross the river bridge, but go over the ladder stile directly at the corner, and along the embankment top path, with the river – the Afon y Glyn – on your left. Carry on to cross the railway and continue ahead. Portmeirion on the opposite side of the Dwyryd Estuary is now in view. At the next stile, cross and go LEFT to the footbridge over the Afon y Glyn. Go over and to the embankment, and go RIGHT alongside it. You are now approaching the hamlet of Ynys. The tall building ahead (Ty Gwyn Mawr) was originally a warehouse. Ynys acted as the port for Harlech. Small ships would reach it, likely to be delivering coal and lime (there was a lime kiln at Llechollwyn). This area was also one of the various places along the estuary where boats were built, and was the landing for the ferry crossing from Porthmadog which, of course, discontinued soon after the railway and road bridge opened at Pont Briwett in 1867. Go out into the road and turn RIGHT along it. There is a choice of seats at two locations when you reach the estuary. Firstly, at the end of this first straight section of road, second, a short distance further along the road on the rocks where the road ends at the next property Llechollwyn. Whichever your choice, it is certainly worth stopping to enjoy the birds and the views. Portmeirion is opposite. Far left, two miles away, at sea level across the estuary is Borth-y-Gest. To the right, looking up the estuary the mountains are the Moelwyns, and further right, some of the foothills of the Rhinog range and just a glimpse of the tops of some of the Rhinog mountains in the far background. A memorial plaque on one of the seats describes this as a special place, and who could disagree.

**2** If you have not yet done so, continue along the road to its end at Llechollwyn. Continue ahead in the same direction, but now walking on the estuary grass. Your precise route can be determined by the state of the tide, and it can be interesting weaving between the small pools. The driest route is to keep up left, close to the exposed dipping rock and the line of trees above it. Whatever your route, eventually get to a large house (Mor Edrin) about ½ mile along the estuary, sited just up from the marsh area. At this house, go to a low stone wall at the edge of the marshland and walk RIGHT along it to a ladder stile in the trees near a gate.

**3** Cross the stile and go ahead to a rough surfaced track at the property Clogwyn-melyn. Go LEFT along the track for about ¼

14

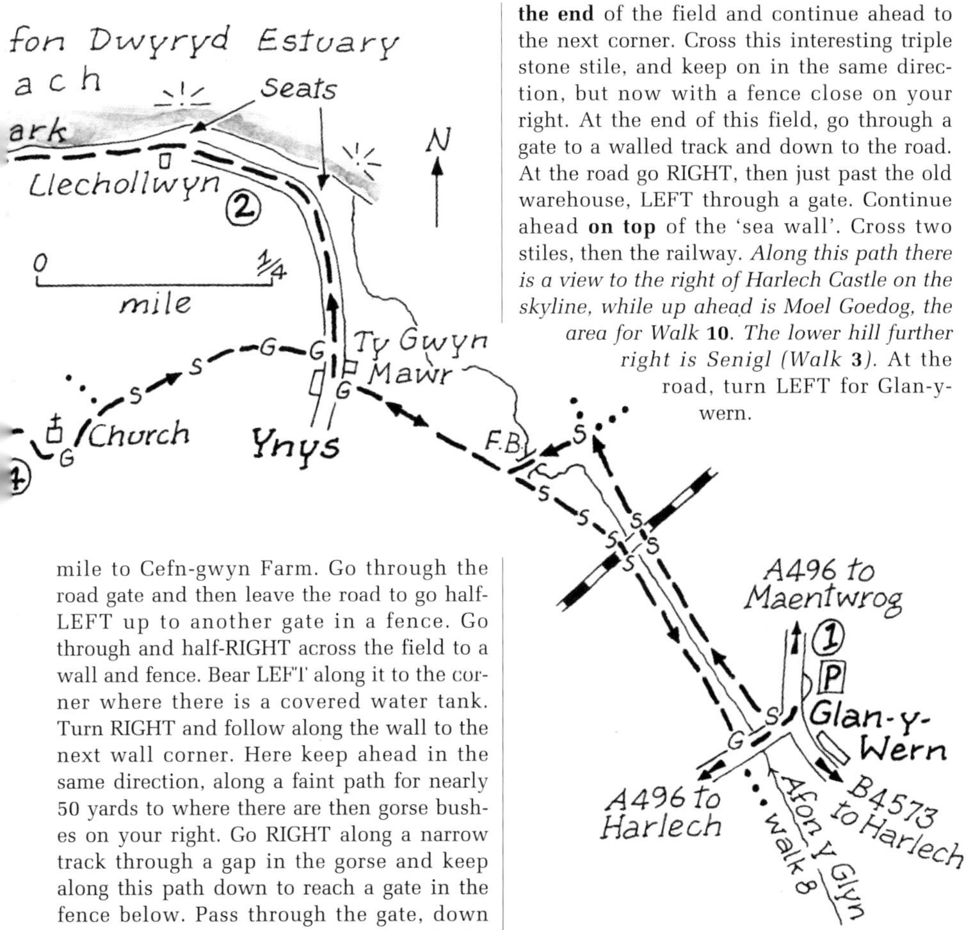

# WALK 7

the end of the field and continue ahead to the next corner. Cross this interesting triple stone stile, and keep on in the same direction, but now with a fence close on your right. At the end of this field, go through a gate to a walled track and down to the road. At the road go RIGHT, then just past the old warehouse, LEFT through a gate. Continue ahead **on top** of the 'sea wall'. Cross two stiles, then the railway. *Along this path there is a view to the right of Harlech Castle on the skyline, while up ahead is Moel Goedog, the area for Walk* **10**. *The lower hill further right is Senigl (Walk 3).* At the road, turn LEFT for Glan-y-wern.

mile to Cefn-gwyn Farm. Go through the road gate and then leave the road to go half-LEFT up to another gate in a fence. Go through and half-RIGHT across the field to a wall and fence. Bear LEFT along it to the corner where there is a covered water tank. Turn RIGHT and follow along the wall to the next wall corner. Here keep ahead in the same direction, along a faint path for nearly 50 yards to where there are then gorse bushes on your right. Go RIGHT along a narrow track through a gap in the gorse and keep along this path down to reach a gate in the fence below. Pass through the gate, down steps and up the other side to reach the church wall.

**4** Go RIGHT along it to the church entrance. *This is 'St. Michael's on the shores' at Llanfihangel-y-traethau, probably on an island when first built, but becoming permanently linked to the mainland when the embankment between Glan-y-wern (where you started), and the Ynys warehouse was built in 1805. There is a note about the church at the door, and an interesting 12th century pillar gravestone closeby.* On leaving the churchyard turn LEFT and go through the signed gate. Follow around the church wall to a wall and fence. Turn RIGHT and walk with it on your left. Cross the stile **at**

'Ty Gwyn Mawr' – the old warehouse at Ynys

15

## WALK 8
# AFON Y GLYN

**DESCRIPTION** A moderate 4 mile walk mainly along the deep narrow valley of the Afon y Glyn, the quietest and least well known of the river valleys near Harlech. A section through woodland is uphill, but rewarded with magnificent views from along the level open track afterwards.

**START** At Glan-y-wern, using a layby just beyond the hamlet, along the east side of the A496, at SH 606349.

**DIRECTIONS** Go north from Harlech along the B4573 (or the A496 if more convenient). After nearly 4 miles, at the junction of the 'A' and 'B' roads at Glan-y-wern, park in the layby just beyond (north) of the road junction (NOT, please, the layby with the telephone box in front of the houses).

**1** For safety reasons, from the layby go back (south) towards Harlech and the Glan-y-wern houses. When just past the road junction cross over the 'B' road, go back to the junction and turn LEFT to cross the river (the Afon y Glyn), and take the signed riverside footpath LEFT. Pass soon through two gates and continue on to reach the road. Go LEFT over the bridge and then RIGHT, along a minor road to reach, in about 200 yards, the cottage, Gefail y Cwm, on your left. Take the signed path through the gate, passing alongside the cottage and on through another gate and up a wide path ahead. *You are now in the quiet valley of the Afon y Glyn, where it runs for about 2 miles in a straight north-east/south-west direction. It is the least frequented of the valleys of the four rivers which start along the Rhinog mountains range and drain westwards to the coast, each of which has a markedly different character and which can be discovered by the walks in this book.* At the top of the rise keep straight ahead, as waymarked, into the trees. After about 100 yards, where the wide track divides, go half-LEFT downhill, staying on the broad track. The track passes an open field on the right and divides again as it enters woodland. Keep ahead RIGHT, walking slightly uphill and carrying on until a road is reached.

**2** Cross the stile into the road, go LEFT, then immediately RIGHT over a stile and up the path LEFT into the wood. At a wall, go through the gate and continue up. *This is an historic path. The few laid steps and stone slabs over small watercourses are old and no doubt assisted the walk to the chapel on the opposite side of the valley from the scattered farmhouses up ahead on this side.* At the end of the wood go over the stone step-stile and on half-RIGHT to a yellow top post at a small group of trees. Go through a wall gap and over a stile. Carry on ahead up through a gap in the rocks and to the farm Tyn y Bwlch. Go out through a gate and then LEFT in front of the farm along the wide track. *It is certainly worth stopping at the top of the rocky outcrop ahead for the views north. From the east (right) the mountains are the Moelwyns, Cnicht, Snowdon, Hebog and the Nantlle Ridge in the background, with the town of Penrhyndeudraeth and Portmeirion on the Dwyryd Estuary nearer.* Continue along the track, through a gate and Cae'n-y-bwlch comes into view.

**3** When at the house, go a few yards RIGHT up the concrete track, then LEFT at a waymark post and down over a wall at the next waymark 40 yards ahead. Carry on down to between trees, one of which has a waymark. At it, go LEFT to a wall gap and past another waymark. Stay on this track down along the wall, **ignoring the gaps** in it, to a ladder stile at the bottom. Go over and ahead half-RIGHT passing to the right of and slightly above hawthorn trees and boulders, and towards a rock outcrop. At the far end of this outcrop bear slightly LEFT down towards a wall and a fence. Go RIGHT along the fence keeping just outside the trees and along the edge of a deep wooded ravine. *The mountain, Cnicht, 6 miles away to the north,* is soon directly ahead of you. The path drops down to a small gate. Go through and down. At the bottom turn LEFT, soon passing to the right of the property Glanrafon. *This property, now one house, was originally three cottages, built for miners who walked to work at*

# WALK 8

Blaenau Ffestiniog and who stayed there during the week. Continue past the house over a six-slab bridge and ahead to the valley road.

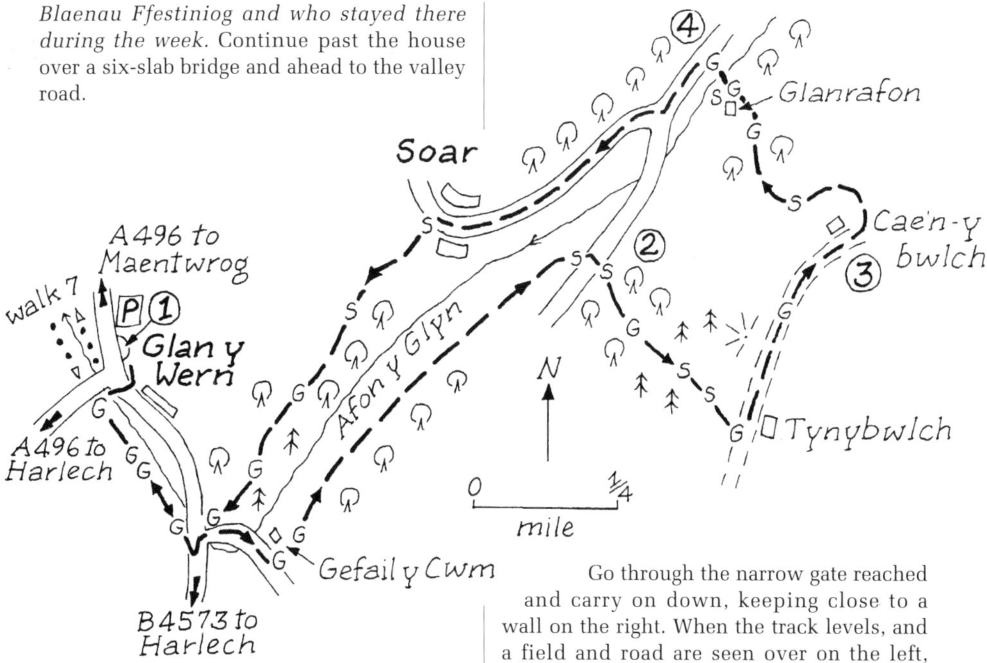

**4** Turn LEFT along the road and RIGHT at the junction in ¼ mile. Continue on this road up to the hamlet Soar. About 100 yards past the last house on the left, go LEFT over the stile and ahead along the path. It soon bears slightly RIGHT to the top of a mound and ahead along the top. At the end, drop down towards a wall and gate. **Ignore and pass** the gate, and carry on with the wall on your left. Keep along this wall and go over the stile at the end. Go half-LEFT ahead. When a wall is seen on the left carry on ahead with the wall on your left. It eventually curves right and there is soon a gate. Go through, half-LEFT down and on ahead to trees and through a gap in a low wall. Keep on in the same general direction through trees with a wall over on the left.

Go through the narrow gate reached and carry on down, keeping close to a wall on the right. When the track levels, and a field and road are seen over on the left, drop down LEFT into the field and curve RIGHT towards a gate onto the road. Turn LEFT along the road, over the bridge, and then RIGHT along the riverside path back to the start.

*Gefail y Cwm*

## WALK 9
# BRYN CADER FANER

**DESCRIPTION** A 6 mile moderate walk starting from a beautifully situated lake, continuing through woodland into an extensive open area of wild beauty, and to the site of a very distinctive Bronze Age stone circle. The central section of this walk, in open countryside, has few landmarks and the walk should not be undertaken in low cloud or mist. Keep it for a fine day for the best rewards.

**START** Alongside the minor road at Llyn Tecwyn Isaf at SH 630371.

**DIRECTIONS** Go about 5 miles north from Harlech along either the 'A' or 'B' roads to Talsarnau. Just beyond the village turn sharp right along the road signed Soar and Llandecwyn. In **100 yards** take the partly concealed road left signed Llandecwyn. At a T-junction in just over a mile, turn left, then at the junction ¼ mile ahead, go right. Park alongside this road at the lake.

**1** Carry on along the road going around to the east side of the lake. About ¼ mile after it leaves the lake go RIGHT at a road junction. In another 200 yards, where the road divides, go LEFT through the gate signed Caerwych. Continue up this road. At the first sharp right turn uphill, Harlech Castle can be seen 5 miles away. Go past Caerwych farmhouse and continue along the road through a wooded valley. This road later opens out into extensive open moorland. The large rectangular stone building on the left was associated with a nearby copper mine. Carry on along the road, past the interesting ruins of a fine barn on the right and on to reach the property, Nant Pasgan-bach.

**2** Here go RIGHT at the signed track. Do NOT then go left through a wall gap but keep ahead, with the remaining section of wall on your left. Maintain this direction, aiming uphill towards the pass in the hills ahead, and soon getting close to a low wall on the right. You should now be on a faint wide track. Keep on it as it goes left around a large rocky outcrop and continues up towards the pass. Stay on this track. It bends left and goes towards the small ravine on the left. Further up the track divides. Keep LEFT on the main track across the now shallow ravine. It soon goes sharp RIGHT, up again towards the pass. Nearer the top the track again curves back left but soon sharply RIGHT. When the track eventually reaches its **highest point** and starts to descend, leave it and go RIGHT, directly to a ladder stile. At the stile there are fine views back. The small lake, a mile away north, is Llyn Llenyrch; the mountains immediately behind it are the Moelwyns.

**3** It is important now to follow these walk directions accurately. Cross the stile and go partly RIGHT ahead towards a pointed rocky outcrop about 100 yards away. Pass close to the LEFT of this outcrop and continue on, same direction, up to the ridge ahead just left of a boggy reed area. Keep ahead on the same course, still keeping left of the large flat boggy area. When this reed area extends left across your route, go partly LEFT up to a large fin-shaped rock about 4 feet high. When you reach it, you will see that it is more than one rock. Just beyond these rocks, is a faint track which can be seen running to the right (south-west) and around the right side of a low mound. Go along this track. The track is part of a prehistoric trackway thought to run from near Llanbedr on the coast to near Trawsfynydd. It is wonderfully rich in standing stones and evidence of ancient settlements, and it continued in use into Medieval times, being one of the important routes linking trading centres at Harlech and Bala. After about 150 yards the track goes between two large mounds about 50 yards apart. The one on the right has much rock outcrop. Here the track divides, the one going left being a modern farm vehicle route. Take the track half-RIGHT, maybe losing sight of it going over boggy ground, but aim to **pass close to the end of the quartz-streaked, rocky mound on the right**. You will cross a narrow boggy stream. The track ahead then becomes more clear. About 200 yards after the quartz rocks there is a small

# WALK 9

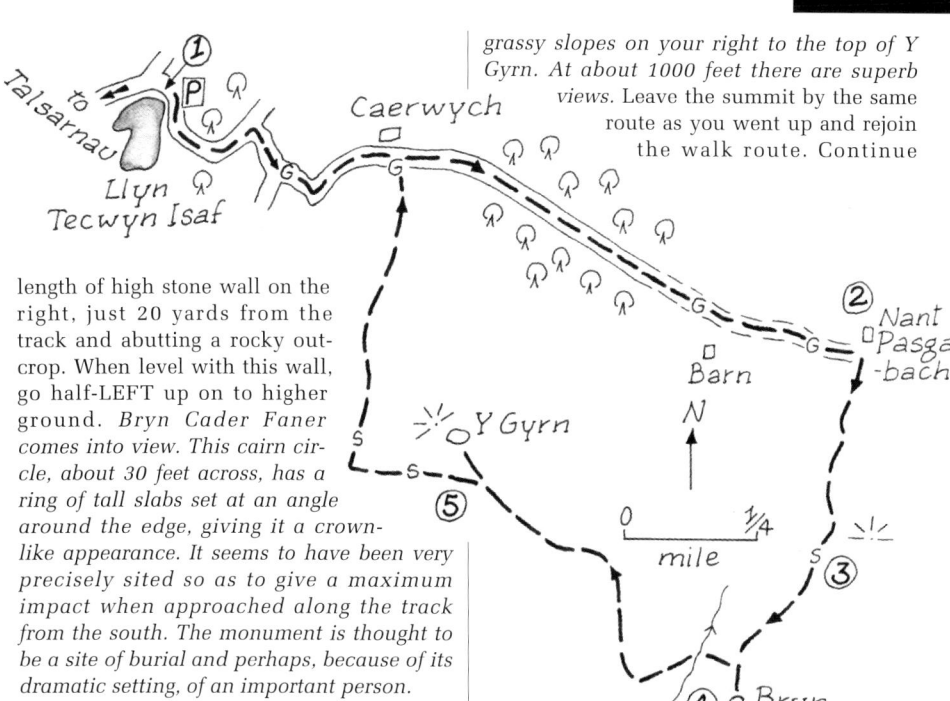

grassy slopes on your right to the top of Y Gyrn. At about 1000 feet there are superb views. Leave the summit by the same route as you went up and rejoin the walk route. Continue

length of high stone wall on the right, just 20 yards from the track and abutting a rocky outcrop. When level with this wall, go half-LEFT up on to higher ground. *Bryn Cader Faner comes into view. This cairn circle, about 30 feet across, has a ring of tall slabs set at an angle around the edge, giving it a crown-like appearance. It seems to have been very precisely sited so as to give a maximum impact when approached along the track from the south. The monument is thought to be a site of burial and perhaps, because of its dramatic setting, of an important person.*

**4** **Return** back down to the track again level with the wall **where you left it**. Continue LEFT along the track, but in 50 yards, go RIGHT, down a steep grassy slope, step across a small stream in the driest looking area, and then ahead up the easiest gradient section of grass slope. **At the first crest**, go half-LEFT towards a large rectangular boulder on the sky line. **At the base** of the last steep climb up to that rock, a clear wide track is reached at right angles to your route. Go RIGHT along this track. *Looking back from here, Bryn Cader Faner can be seen again.* In about 50 yards, the track divides. Keep RIGHT – it can be seen ahead where it is rock supported as it curves right. Stay along this track. When a large flat boggy area is reached the track itself becomes increasingly difficult to follow. It is best to keep on the right edge of this extensive flat area, close to the gorse covered slopes on the right. Continue around, but do not leave the flat area. *When at the far end of the flat area, just as Portmeirion and the estuary below come into view, and before your route starts to drop down, it is well worth going up the*

along the base of the gorse slopes on your right. Below Y Gyrn, the track now goes steeply down.

**5** At the bottom wall, go over the stile on the left. Go half-RIGHT ahead, down through a wall gap. Keep along the track down, and near the bottom go RIGHT, over to the low walls of an old rectangular structure 50 yards away. From here, go RIGHT to reach a ladder stile over a wall 75 yards away. Cross, and continue ahead with the wall on your left. In about 200 yards go LEFT through a wide gap in the wall (sometimes a gate). Go half-RIGHT along a track but **in just 25 yards** go LEFT, slightly down and along the edge of the reeds. This leads to a clear wide track. *Llyn Tecwyn Isaf soon appears down to the left ahead.* Keep along this track through two wall gaps (or gates?) to Caerwych Farm. Turn LEFT along the road and follow it back to the lake.

## WALK 10
# AROUND MOEL GOEDOG

**DESCRIPTION** An easy 5½ mile walk in open countryside with outstanding views, and along an easy-to-follow track. There is much of prehistoric interest.

**START** An open area alongside the minor road from Llanfair to Eisingrug, at SH 603316.

**DIRECTIONS** From Harlech go south to the Llanfair/Llandanwg crossroads on the A496. Turn left (east) and then left again at the next crossroads in ¼ mile. In another ¼ mile go right at the signed 'Cwm Bychan 6' junction. Stay on this road for about 3 miles to the entrance to Merthyr Farm, which is on the left about ¼ mile after crossing a cattle grid. Park (the landowner has kindly given permission) in the open area on the right. Please be careful not to block gates or hinder farm vehicles using the Merthyr Farm entrance.

**1** Leave the parking area and continue north along the road. After nearly ½ mile, at a footpath sign, leave the road and take the track half-RIGHT. In about 100 yards the track divides. Take the LEFT fork and go through the gate 100 yards ahead. Carry on and through the next gate, and along the green track ahead. *The hill on your right is Moel Goedog, and at about 1200 feet, there are outstanding all round views from the top. If you wish to go up, there is a gap in the fence about 100 yards after the gate. At the top are the remains of an ancient hillfort, now divided by three stone walls. However, there are ladder stiles which allow those interested to examine the whole site.* **To continue the walk from the top** go over the stile on your left as you reach the top, and walk down that field to rejoin the track, and go RIGHT along it. **If you have stayed on the track**, in about another 50 yards after the fence gap, and just after the track starts to go slightly down, there is a Bronze Age burial ring cairn on the left. Continue along the track, through the next gate and on to go through another gate. *There are now superb views across the Dwyryd estuary and further north to the high mountains of the National Park. If the views make you want to stay longer in this area, it is possible to go to a secluded lake (Llyn y Fedw) by taking a faint track RIGHT just after going past a low wall about 300 yards after the last gate.*

**2** The walk continues along the main track, eventually reaching a ladder stile in a wall ahead. Cross and carry on to the next wall and ladder stile in about 300 yards. Go ahead, with a wall down on your left but which later comes up close to the path. Where it does, at a bend right in the path, a more remote and wilder peat-dominated area comes into view ahead with the mountains Ysgyfarnogod (just over 2000 feet) and, to the right, Clip, in the background. It is across this area that a Bronze Age trackway continues, and which is thought to have started near Llanbedr and taken the route of this walk so far. You may have noticed a number of standing stones along the road to the parking area, and afterwards, possibly to help indicate the easiest route in those times, along higher drier ground than the marshes below. Continue now with the wall close on your left and reach a ladder stile with a low waymark post. The path over the stile continues along the ancient track, but for this walk follow the blue waymark ahead, keeping the wall on your left and best taking a faint path about 20 yards from it. After about 100 yards a tractor track (which has been in the tall grass close to the wall) is reached as it swings away from the wall. Go RIGHT along this track, up over the low ridge and down, curving right, to reach another blue waymark. Turn RIGHT as indicated along a similar green track and over a ladder stile at the next wall.

# WALK 10

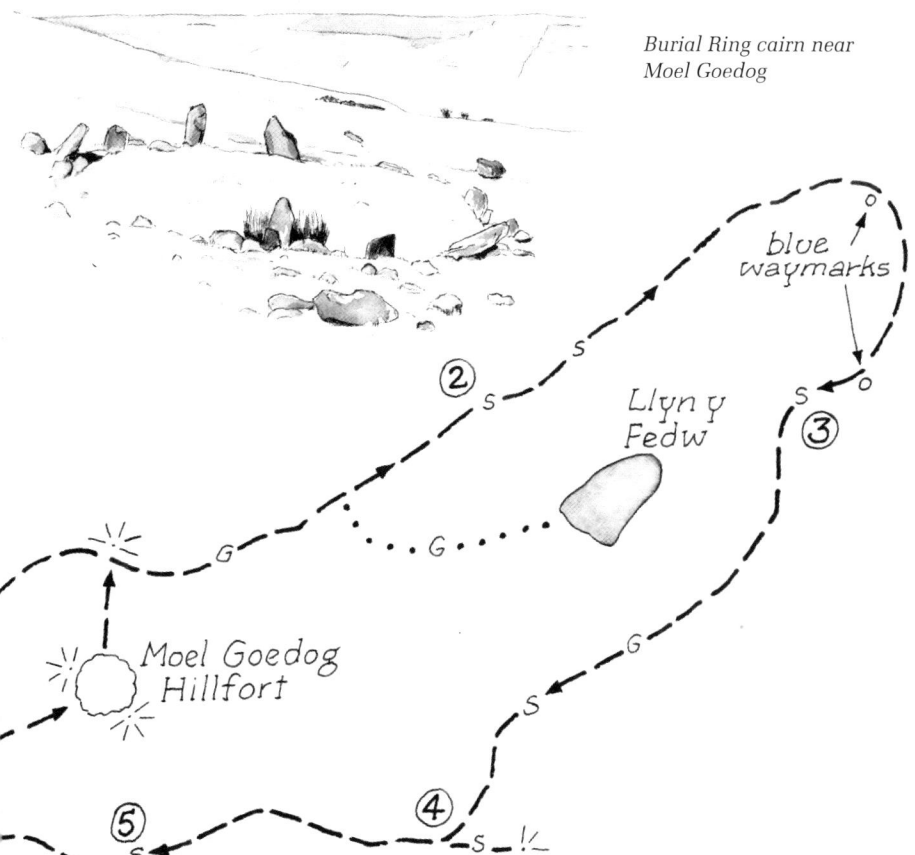

*Burial Ring cairn near Moel Goedog*

**3** Keep along this track, going through a gap in the next wall and now with a wall on your left. Reach a gate and go through along the track. It goes through a wall gap and on down to another ladder stile in sight ahead. Cross and continue along the track.

**4** After about ¼ mile the track joins another close to a wall ahead, and where there are two ladder stiles nearby. One is ahead and slightly right, the other to the left alongside a gate. Go LEFT and over that stile, and walk to the top of the small mound ahead next to a wall on the right. *There are wonderful views into Cwm Bychan, with the lake visible. The high rounded mountain right of the lake is Rhinog Fawr (2362 feet), while over to the left are Clip and Ysgyfarnogod.*

*You can even see Snowdon, well to the north.* Return over the ladder stile and continue along the clear track from it with a wall on your left. **Ignore** the stile over that wall and continue ahead to another ladder stile in about ½ mile.

**5** Cross and go ahead along the track (rather faint). It soon curves left, and then right where there is a choice of tracks both going down to cross the lowest part of this area. It is best to take the track which is slightly left of the other. (**Note: the ladder stile way over on your left is not on your route.**) At the next wall ahead (the wall coming down from Moel Goedog on the right) the track curves left and goes through two gates and ahead to the road. Turn LEFT for the parking area.

21

## WALK 11
# LLANBEDR WOODLANDS

**DESCRIPTION** An easy 3½ mile beautiful low level walk. It will be appreciated especially by those who enjoy walking in superb natural woodlands.
**START** A little way along the minor road which leaves the A496 at the Victoria Inn, Llanbedr, at SH 585268
**DIRECTIONS** Go south from Harlech on the A496 to Llanbedr. In the village turn left (east) at the Victoria Inn, along the road signed Cwm Bychan and Cwm Nantcol. Park about 150 yards up that road on the left side just before the Ty Mawr Hotel.

**1** Continue along the road (east) away from the village and turn LEFT at the next junction at the war memorial. Go past the houses and on beyond the last cottage, Tan-y-Wenallt. Ignore all footpath signs until, about ½ mile after Tan-y-Wenallt, the next house (Hen Bandy) on the right is reached. At this property go RIGHT, between the house and an outbuilding, up into the wood (the path sign is in the hedge on the left side of the road). After a gate, keep going up along the path slightly right, and after a stony section where a faint path joins from the right, go LEFT keeping along the main path. A surfaced drive at the Ranch (an outdoor discovery centre) is soon reached. Turn LEFT along it, through the car parking area, and out into an open field. Stay on this drive until just before it bears sharply left. Here, go partly back very sharply RIGHT diagonally up a faint path across the open field. Near the top go over LEFT to a stone step-stile in the wall near the top field corner.

**2** Go over, through trees and rocks, into an open area following the path ahead to a wall with a gate and stile. Go through and continue half-LEFT to the next stile visible just over 100 yards ahead. Cross and go straight ahead (**not left**) for 25 yards to the start of a wide path right. Here, the narrow path straight ahead up on to the top of the rock outcrops, and then going slightly right, takes you to an ancient hut circle. However, the walk continues along the wide path RIGHT, passing to the left of a fine oak tree and the back of a former cottage. Keep on down to an interesting metal stile. Cross and carry on ahead, and in about 50 yards, at a junction of walls, keep ahead between two walls to a gate. Go through and follow close to the wall curving LEFT to reach a farm. Pass to the RIGHT of the house and up to a rough surfaced track. Go LEFT along it, down, to cross a cattle grid at a barn. Turn RIGHT through the second gate and go ahead with a wall on your right. A fine view from here, to the right, of Moelfre – the area of Walk 15. Go through the wall gap ahead and along the path half-LEFT. Cross the field, keeping to the right of the boggy area, and close to the trees and a field wall on your right. At a stepped gap in the wall, go through into the wood.

**3** In 25 yards, at a main track, turn RIGHT. Keep along this beautiful woodland track for nearly ½ mile, and go through a small gate. Continue half-LEFT and in about 100 yards reach a waymark post on the left. At this post, a path junction, turn very sharp RIGHT and go down a path in this new direction soon passing old buildings to reach a ladder stile. Go over and keep ahead, passing a waymark, to another stile. Cross and go through the gate ahead and on up to reach a wide rough surfaced track. Go LEFT along this track. Ignore the similar track right after about 100 yards, keeping ahead bearing slightly LEFT, and dropping down. *On this section there are fine views up Cwm Bychan.*

**4** In another 100 yards, as you meet trees and a fence ahead, turn very sharply RIGHT along a similar rough track. Stay on this track going past farm buildings on the right, and passing the house Penrallt, and continuing ahead along a less surfaced track, close to a wall on your left. Go through a gate and continue along the wall. Stay with it when it curves left and drops down to a gate. Go through, down to the road, and go LEFT along it back to Llanbedr.

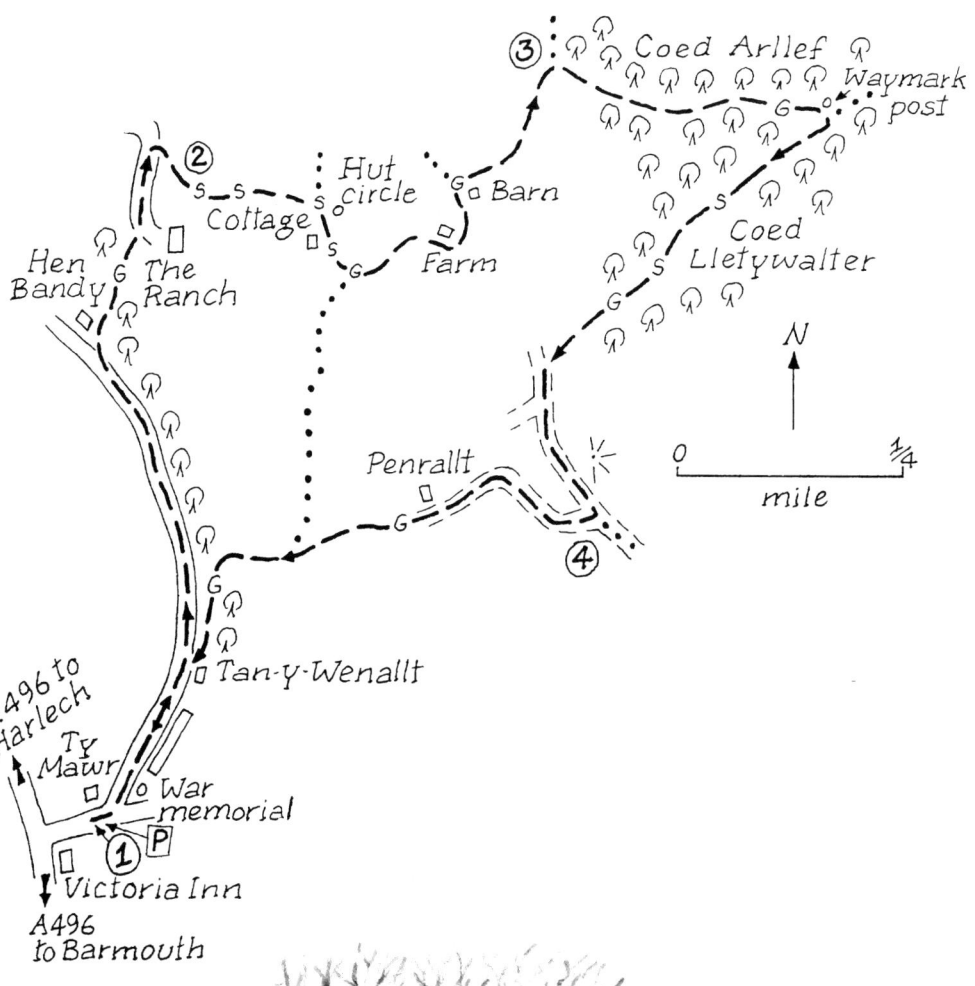

Capel Salem
(Walk 12)

## WALK 12

# CAPEL SALEM & HAFOD Y LLYN

**DESCRIPTION** A 4½ mile easy, low level, walk in mixed and very attractive countryside using some fine walled green lanes, and including a visit to a chapel featured in probably the most famous 'Welsh' painting.

**START** Along the start of the minor road serving Cwm Nantcol, at SH 601272.

**DIRECTIONS** Go south from Harlech on the A496 to Llanbedr. In the village turn left (east) at the Victoria Inn, along the road signed Cwm Bychan and Cwm Nantcol. In just over 1 mile, turn right (signed Cwm Nantcol) to cross the river, then first left. Cross the cattle grid and park on land alongside the river a little way up on the left.

**1** Carry on up the road to Salem Chapel. It is Salem Chapel in which Curnow Vosper painted, in 1908, the picture which has hung in thousands of Welsh homes, and was exhibited at the Royal Academy in 1909. The original, bought later that year by Lord Leverhulme, is in the gallery at Port Sunlight, but a copy is of course in the Chapel. Were it not for the popularity of the painting, Salem would probably not be a chapel of such interest. But it is a fine example of a Baptist chapel, with a plain unpretentious interior where the emphasis was on the 'word'. It was built in 1850. Before that, worshippers met in one of the row of cottages below, where you have parked, and it was the river (the Artro), just below Salem, which was used for baptisms. After visiting, continue on past the Chapel. IGNORE the first footpath sign on the left in 30 yards, but at the second path sign in another 30 yards go LEFT. Go up into a walled track and curve left to reach a gate. Pass through and keep on ahead alongside a wall. At the wall corner carry straight on and through the wall gap directly ahead. Maintain the same direction, eventually reaching a swing gate at the top corner of this large field. Go through and ahead to pass to the left of the property Y Fron.

**2** At the surfaced drive go LEFT along it down to the river bridge at Pen-y-bont. Go RIGHT along the road for 75 yards, then LEFT over the stone step-stile. Follow along the wall on your left to the way-marked stile ahead. Cross and go half-RIGHT to the farm barns. Go through the gate just beyond the first barn, go RIGHT and through another gate, and over a cattle grid to a road.

**3** Go straight across and through a gate. At the end of the wall on your right, go half-RIGHT to reach a small river and the course of an old leat. *This leat served a tannery, the ruins of which are along to the right.* Bear LEFT and through a way-marked gate to follow a route alongside the wall on your left. Go through the gate at the end of the track and bear RIGHT, passing a barn on your left and on to another fine section of walled lane. At the junction ahead turn LEFT. Go through the gate at the end of this length and continue along the track half-RIGHT.

**4** On reaching farm ruins (Blaidd Bwll) turn immediately LEFT after going through the entrance wall gap, and go through another gap. Continue ahead along the ditch and line of trees on your right. In about 100 yards, where the ditch meets a wall coming from the field on the right, and where the ditch is bridged, go LEFT up through a gap in the gorse and bushes. When through into the next field, go sharp LEFT as waymarked, and on to pass to the left of an isolated oak tree and over another bridged ditch. Keep ahead, through a wall gap and then half-RIGHT across to a wall corner. At this corner, do NOT turn left but go up ahead through gorse. The farm Tyddyn Rhyddid comes into view. Bear LEFT to reach a swing gate in the wall below. Go through and ahead, through two more gates close together, and continue ahead along the wall. When a fence is reached ahead, go LEFT along it and out through a gate to the farm drive. Go LEFT, through another gate, to the road.

**5** Turn RIGHT along the road for about 100 yards, then LEFT through a signed gate and along the Penarth Farm drive.

# WALK 12

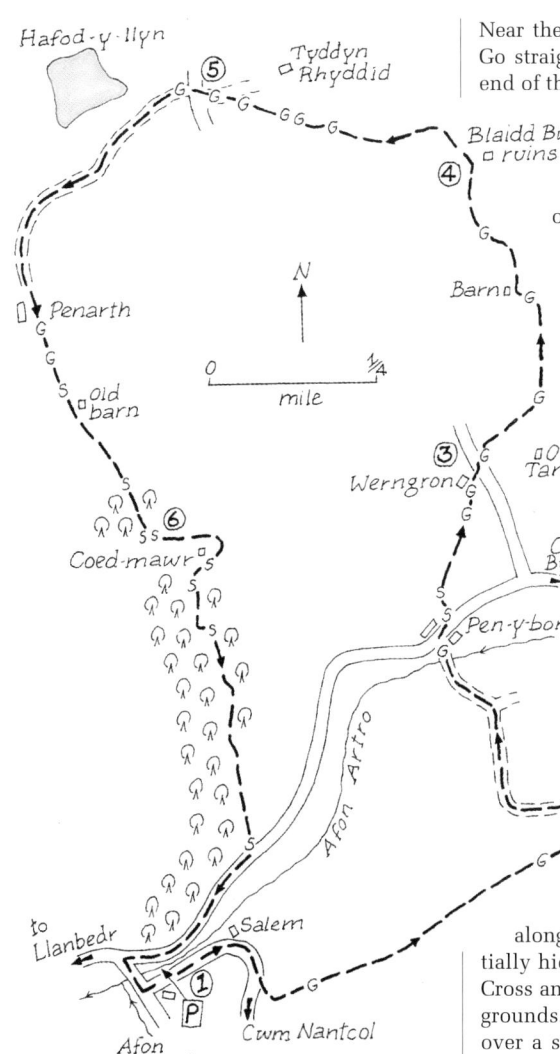

Near the barn cross the stile over the fence. Go straight ahead until level with the gable end of the barn and about 25 yards from it. **It is important to get into this position.** From here go half-LEFT across this rough field, cutting across the line of rock outcroppings, until about 25 yards from the field wall ahead. Then turn half-RIGHT and walk parallel to the wall (probably along one of the rock outcrops) to reach trees in the bottom corner of the field. Find the rather hidden waymarked step-stile in the wall ahead and cross it. Go down through the trees to reach some path signs and two stiles. Cross the fence stile and then go immediately LEFT over the stone step-stile.

**6** Go ahead across the field to pass through a wall gap just left of the buildings (Coed-Mawr). At a waymark post follow the wall around to the RIGHT. When in 20 yards the wall goes further right, keep ahead along the track and down into another field. Here go very sharply back RIGHT, keeping along bushes on your right to reach a partially hidden ladder stile in the field corner. Cross and go through the gate into the house grounds. Then turn LEFT into the wood and over a stile. Follow along the wall on your left and where it later joins another wall and goes right, go LEFT through a wall gap. In a short distance go over the stile in the wall now on your right and continue ahead and down with a wall on your right. At the bottom turn RIGHT along a flat area parallel to a fence on your right. Keeping reasonably close to the fence, drop down to trees below, curving to the right. Carry on, and where a wall appears ahead across your route, bear LEFT and walk with this wall on your right. At a stone step-stile ahead, cross and go RIGHT, along the road back to the start.

Follow this track to the farm. *The lake below on the right, which you can visit, is Hafod-y-llyn.* When the farm buildings are reached take the wide track half-LEFT just before a large modern barn. Go through wide gates beyond the barn and go LEFT, but very shortly slightly RIGHT and down to a track through a gate 50 yards ahead. When, in about 100 yards, an old barn comes clearly into view ahead, leave the track where it curves left and maintain the same direction across the rough ground towards the barn.

## WALK 13
# CARREG FAWR

**DESCRIPTION** This fine walk is included for experienced hill-walkers who enjoy a challenge of route finding in open country. It should **not** be undertaken in low cloud or mist. Although only about 4½ miles and with a straight forward start, it is not all an easy stroll. But it is very rewarding: the beautiful Artro river valley to start, then native woodland, followed at about the 1000 foot level by thick heather and moorland from where there are superb views. Reduction in sheep numbers has helped the heather growth, and it is spectacular when in bloom in August. But it means in some places that an actual path is difficult to find; bracken too can be challenging. In these circumstances our map can usefully be supplemented with the OS map Explorer OL18. There are four key points on the walk which it is essential to reach. They are shown **A**, **B**, **C** and **D** on the map in this book and their grid references are given in the walk directions.

**START** Park along the minor road from Llanbedr to Cwm Bychan at Pont Cwm-yr-afon, at SH 622298 (small charge).

**DIRECTIONS** Go south from Harlech on the A496 to Llanbedr. In the village turn left (east) at the Victoria Inn, along the road signed Cwm Bychan and Cwm Nantcol. At a road junction in just over 1 mile, keep straight ahead along the Cwm Bychan road. In about a further 2 miles park on the right **by the river bridge** (the second, not the first, of two similar riverside parking areas).

**❙** Walk back down the valley road for about ½ mile to Crafnant Farm on your right. In a further 250 yards, go half-LEFT through a gate down to cross the river at Pont Crafnant. Follow the track RIGHT, passing left of an old barn and over a ladder stile. Keep along this track up through the wood. *On your right is the Coed Crafnant Nature Reserve owned by the North Wales Wildlife Trust and described as a fine example of ancient woodland rich in mosses, liverworts and ferns. Well worth a visit on another day.*

Just after this wide stony track ends in an open area, take the grass path half-RIGHT uphill, eventually passing to the left of an old small building. Continue uphill in this open area in the same direction, although a path is not always clear. When the first trees are reached at the top of the open area go RIGHT into the next open area and stay on that course. When the next trees are reached, keep ahead to reach a fence and wall. Go up LEFT along it to a small gate and ladder stile. (This is **A** on the map, at GR 623289, and the first of the four key location points.)

**2** This is the end of the wooded area. Cross the stile and continue uphill, along the track from the gate, and leading roughly east. Stay along this track until it ends at a gap in a low wall. Continue up in the same general direction, sometimes alongside boggy areas and increasingly in heather and perhaps bracken. You will reach a low old wall on your right. DO NOT cross it but keep on the left of it to where it turns sharp left across your route. At this corner, go through and continue up in the same direction. Pass to the right of a heathery mound, and soon a high wall is in sight ahead on the right. Go up towards it, and bear LEFT to reach a wall gap in it. (This is **B** on the map at GR 627291.)

**3** Go through the gap and find a way half-LEFT ahead to go along the right side of a very low line of rocks. A (probably hidden) path further ahead then zig-zags up the slope in front through thick heather. If you cannot find this 'path', make your way up as best you can, keeping the high wall on your left in view. In about 250 yards you will come to a ladder stile high up in the wall on your left. (This is **C** on the map at GR 629292, the third key point.)

**4** Cross and go straight ahead through the heather. In about 20 yards, the narrow path bears right, and there is an even less distinct path going half-LEFT up the slope. Go along it. It soon bears LEFT and goes over exposed rock and continues up. Go up to reach a stone cairn at the very top. *This is Carreg Fawr at about 1000 feet, and there*

# WALK 13

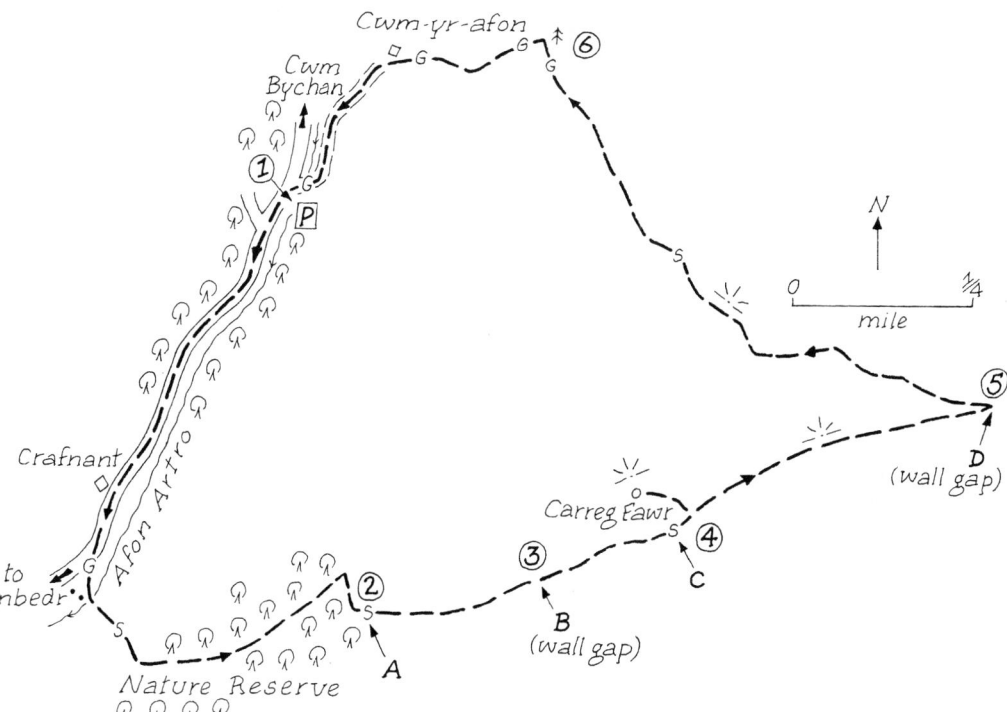

are superb all-around views. When you must leave, go back down the route you came up and rejoin the path from the ladder stile. Go LEFT (roughly north-eastwards) across the moorland. Some small tracks are visible, and after about 200 yards you should be walking roughly parallel to a wall up on your right, and then gradually getting closer to it. It is easy walking at first, but after about ¼ mile the terrain becomes more difficult and probably with no clear path. Depending on conditons underfoot, you might deviate (perhaps going slightly left and lower around some of the hummocks) and so may not always have the wall on your right in sight. However, keep it generally in view because you will be approaching and need to locate the clear gap in the wall at GR 637294. (This is key point **D** on the map.) It is found just after the wall drops steeply down.

**5** This wall gap is where an old mineral track passes through to former workings up ahead. DO NOT go through the gap, but go back, westwards, along and down the track. Near the beginning the track is boggy but later becomes much drier. Keep on this track for nearly a mile as it drops down to the valley bottom. *There are glorious views all the way.* At one point, after about ½ mile, where the track levels out at a wall on the left, go to the ladder stile across the grass ahead to the right, and NOT through the gates on the left. Pick up the track again soon after crossing the stile – it is at the end of the wall on your left – and continue down.

**6** Go through the gate at the bottom and straight ahead to join another track just past the trees. Turn LEFT to the next gate and stay along the track ahead. Continue on through another gate, and pass to the left of Cwm-yr-afon Farm. Bear LEFT along the farm track back to the start.

## WALK 14
# CWM NANTCOL

**DESCRIPTION** A moderate 6 mile walk partly along the valley floor and partly up on the northern slopes. Wonderful views in open countryside. It is a walk which allows a fine appreciation of this beautiful valley.

**START** Along the minor road serving Cwm Nantcol from Llanbedr, at Capel Nantcol. SH 623262

**DIRECTIONS** Go south from Harlech on the A496 to Llanbedr. In the village turn left (east) at the Victoria Inn, along the road signed Cwm Bychan and Cwm Nantcol. In just over 1 mile, turn right (signed Cwm Nantcol) to cross the river, then first left. In a further 2 miles at Capel Nantcol (where there are a telephone box and a post box on the right) park in the space on the left.

**1** From the parking area take the adjacent signed path through a gate down towards the river (north). Shortly, go through another gate and turn RIGHT along a wall. At the next gate in the wall and by a waymark post, go LEFT to reach a waymark post 75 yards ahead. **Because of the drainage ditches in the valley, often hidden from view, it is important to follow the walk directions very carefully, otherwise the small bridges across them may not be found.** Continue in the same northerly direction across the rough grass to another waymark post in about 75 yards where a drainage ditch is bridged. Keep again in the same direction ahead to the next waymark post, at the river, and turn RIGHT to a footbridge.

**2** Cross and go straight ahead with a drainage ditch on your left. In 30 yards, curve LEFT aiming towards a small spur of rock outcrop jutting into the valley floor. Follow, on your left, another ditch, and go to the low waymark post just left of the rock spur. Here cross the slab bridge and go half-RIGHT to another waymark 100 yards ahead. Continue ahead to a yellow-top post in another 100 yards. Here go RIGHT (to two posts at a footbridge) and alongside a ditch on your left, up to a wide gate and old farm buildings.

**3** Go through the gate, up to the left of the buildings, and on up an old track. Cross over the stile at a fence and go LEFT along a wide track. Keep along this track until, in nearly ½ mile, it joins a road. Go LEFT and carry on to the main valley road. Here, go RIGHT, and about 100 yards after the **second** house (Gelliwaen) turn RIGHT up a wide rough track, passing to the side of a gate, and continuing up for ¼ mile to another gate.

**4** Go through, and then RIGHT along a wide grass track. *There are soon fine views over the valley. Keep a look out for wild goats.* The track curves left, and after a long straight stretch uphill it curves again slightly left. 50 yards after this bend, at a path junction, take the **partially concealed** similar grass track half-RIGHT. After 200 yards, cross a stile and continue along the track. At the next wall go through the gate and ahead. Go through another gate in about 300 yards and continue with a wall on your left. Go over the ladder stile at the next wall and LEFT along the wall. **Ignore** the ladder stile and gate in the wall on your left after 250 yards, and continue on to reach a gate in a wall **across** your route in about another 75 yards. Go through and ahead along the track keeping along it as it later curves slightly to the right, away from the wall, and passing to the left of an area of large rocks. As the track approaches the last, rather isolated, higher rock outcrop, follow it RIGHT and on through a wall gap. Stay on the track up to a ladder stile and gate in a wall 200 yards ahead. *The trench up on the left is the line of former manganese workings, much evidence of which will be seen along this section of the walk.* Go over the stile and ahead along the lower (right) of the two tracks leading from the gate. When another ladder stile comes into view work partly LEFT to cross it. Keep ahead along this old mineral track. In 150 yards, you reach the ruins of a small stone building on the right. **Care in following the route directions is needed here.** 75 yards after this building, at the top of a slight rise you will see the built-up pathway, slightly

# WALK 14

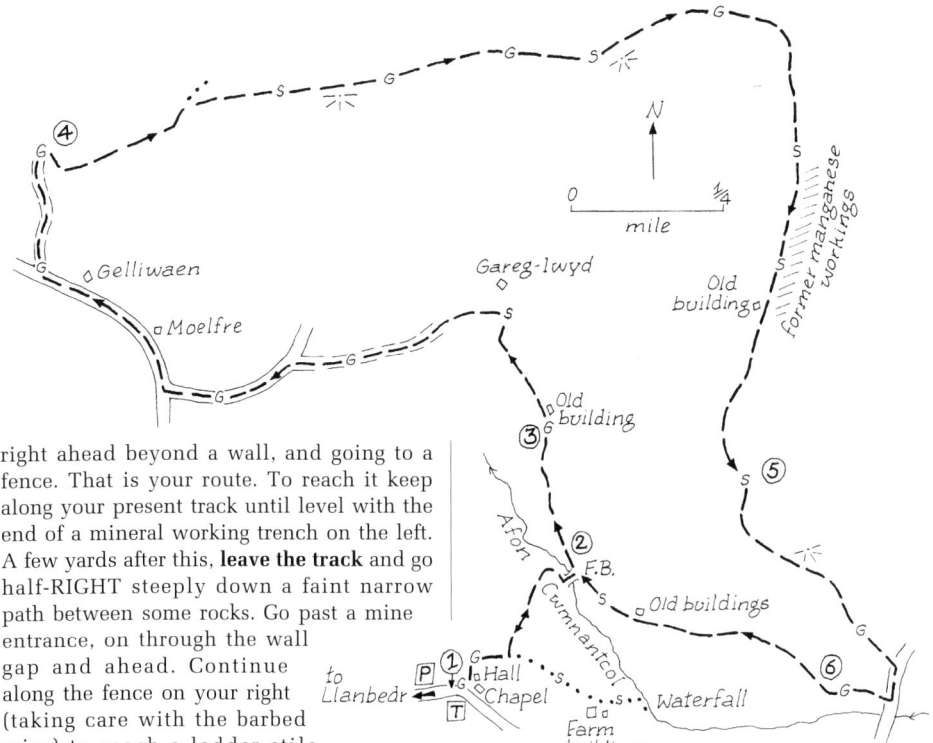

right ahead beyond a wall, and going to a fence. That is your route. To reach it keep along your present track until level with the end of a mineral working trench on the left. A few yards after this, **leave the track** and go half-RIGHT steeply down a faint narrow path between some rocks. Go past a mine entrance, on through the wall gap and ahead. Continue along the fence on your right (taking care with the barbed wire) to reach a ladder stile. Cross and go down ahead.

**5** Soon the grass topped Y Llethr, the highest of the Rhinog range at 2475 feet is directly ahead. Flat topped Rhinog Fach is to its left. Across the valley to the right is Moelfre, the core of Walk **15**. Keep on down, through a narrow wall gap, ahead across sloping rock surfaces to a gate in a wall below on the left. Go through and along the path ahead, then RIGHT through a wall gap in 100 yards and half-LEFT to the road. Go RIGHT, and RIGHT again at the footpath sign just **before** the road bridge. Cross the field to the gate 100 yards ahead.

**6** Go through into this geologically very interesting area and half-LEFT across rock slabs. Follow the path as it curves right, through a small wall gap and on to a waymark post. Follow the arrow exactly and go partly up the end of the sloping rock and slightly LEFT along a faint path to keep up from the boggy area on the left. Go to the next waymark now visible. Carry on as indicated using the four more waymarks placed at intervals of about 100 yards, eventually dropping down to the valley floor at a waymarked wall gap. Go across to a yellow-top post and continue on, passing to the left of old buildings, to some trees. Here go half-RIGHT as indicated, to a ladder stile. Cross and go ahead, soon with a drainage ditch on your left, to the footbridge. Cross and turn RIGHT. At the waymark post ahead go LEFT to the next one and on to reach the wall ahead. At the wall you have a choice. Turn RIGHT to get back to the start. *However to visit a nearby fine waterfall and pool (in ¼ mile), go LEFT along the wall to farm buildings about 300 yards ahead. At the farm go half-LEFT across a field to a ladder stile. Cross and go ahead to the waterfall. Return the same way.*

## WALK 15
# AROUND MOELFRE

**DESCRIPTION** An easy 5½ mile walk around the base of the rounded 1900 foot hill, Moelfre, 5 miles south of Harlech, and which stands detached from the nearby Rhinog range of mountains. It is a walk in open country with outstanding views, providing a chance to sample the expansive wildness of the Ysgethin valley, and to give thought to the stagecoaches that crossed it in the 18th century.

**START** Along the minor road passing on the north side of Moelfre at SH 614258.

**DIRECTIONS** Go south from Harlech along the A496 for about 5 miles to Dyffryn Ardudwy. Before the village centre, and about ½ mile after passing the 30 mph signs, take the road left (east) signed 'Cwm Nantcol 3½'. At a skewed crossroads in 1½ miles, go right then immediately left (Cwm Nantcol). In another mile park on the left in an open area just past an old quarry on the right.

**1** Walk back along the road (south-westerly) towards the sea. *In about ¼ mile, at a swing gate on your right, visit Ffynnon Enddwyn, an ancient well said to have curative properties. A board at the well tells you more.* After another ¼ mile, take the signed wide track LEFT up across open country. This leads to a corner where four walls meet. Go through the gate and small sheep pen and go RIGHT, parallel to a wall on the right. *The undulations up on your left are the results of manganese mining which ceased about 100 years ago.* Keep along the wall and go through a gate at the end of the field. Carry on in the same direction with the wall on the right and go through another gate. Continue ahead and reach a footpath sign at a wide track. Go LEFT along it and soon through a gate. *This is part of the old coach road from Bontddu to Llanbedr. The smooth slopes of Moelfre are up on your left.*

**2** After about ½ mile go through another gate and join a rough-surfaced wide track. Go LEFT along it. *The wild landscape of the Ysgethin valley is soon in full view. On your right, the rocky spur jutting out into the valley floor from the slopes of Moelfre is topped at the end by Craig y Dinas, a prehistoric small defensive enclosure. Further on, after going beyond the top of the spur, the parapets of the 17th or 18th century bridge, Pont Scethin, down on your right, will just be seen. On your left, the ruins just beyond the conifer trees are of a coaching inn, a reminder that the old coach road between Harlech and Bontddu crossed this valley, there being no possible route then via Barmouth. That route was not carved out of rock until 1798.* Stay along this rough surfaced track. Nearly ¼ mile past the end of the conifer trees, and clear of the last of the outcropping of rocks on the steep lower slopes of Moelfre on the left, you reach a position on the track which is nearly level with the lowest section of the grassy, gentler, ridge of moorland up on the left. Leave the track at this point and go LEFT over rough grass up towards the ridge. *When about half-way up, there is a fine last sweeping view back of the whole length of the Ysgethin valley.*

**3** Near the top of the ridge, if you come to a vehicular grass track across your route, go LEFT along it, and bearing RIGHT where it forks very near the top, to reach a gate. If you miss this track, keep on going up and at the top of the ridge, look left for the wall coming down steeply from the summit of Moelfre. Go towards the point where it starts to level out and to the gate. soon seen in the wall. Go through and follow the path ahead and down, through a gap in the next wall, and on through another in the following wall. *The views now far ahead are across Tremadog Bay to the Lleyn Peninsula, while close ahead is Cwm Nantcol and, half-right, the rocky mass of Rhinog Fawr. Soon, more spectacular views open up to the right, revealing Rhinog Fach and the pass Bwlch Drws-Ardudwy between Fawr and Fach, and also the grassy top of Y Llethr, at 2475 feet the highest of the Rhinog range.* Continue down, through a third wall gap and over a stile at the next wall. From here the track goes half-LEFT, then RIGHT, alongside an

# WALK 15

Pont Scethin

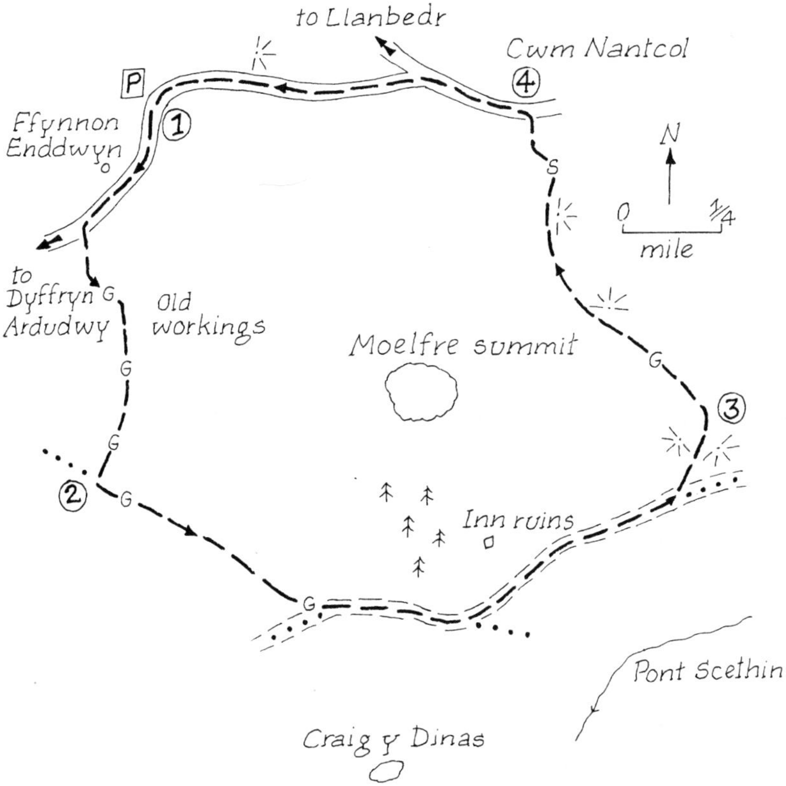

old low wall and down to the valley road.

**4** At the road go LEFT, and in ¼ mile LEFT again at the next road junction (signed Dyffryn Ardudwy). This quiet road takes you back to the start. *Enjoy the fine views back (east) up Cwm Nantcol. Opposite, across the valley (north), can be seen the hillsides of Walk* **14**.

## PRONUNCIATION

These basic points should help non-Welsh speakers

| Welsh | English equivalent |
|---|---|
| c | always hard, as in **c**at |
| ch | as in the Scottish word lo**ch** |
| dd | as th in **th**en |
| f | as v in **v**ocal |
| ff | as **f** |
| g | always hard as in **g**ot |
| ll | no real equivalent. It is like 'th' in **th**en, but with an 'L' sound added to it, giving '**thlan**' for the pronunciation of the Welsh 'Llan'. |

In Welsh the accent usually falls on the last-but-one syllable of a word.

## KEY TO THE MAPS

- →   Walk route and direction
- ═   Metalled road
- ---   Unsurfaced road
- ....   Footpath/route adjoining walk route
- ~~~   River/stream
- ♣ ♧   Trees
- ■■■   Railway
- **G**   Gate
- **S**   Stile
- F.B.   Footbridge
- ⊻⊻   Viewpoint
- [P]   Parking
- [T]   Telephone

## THE COUNTRY CODE

Enjoy the countryside and respect its life and work

Guard against all risk of fire

Leave gates *as you find them*

Keep your dogs under close control

Keep to public paths across farmland

Use gates and stiles to cross fences, hedges and walls

Leave livestock, crops and machinery alone

Take your litter home

Help to keep all water clean

Protect wildlife, plants and trees

Take special care on country roads

Make no unnecessary noise

---

Published by
**Kittiwake** 3 Glantwymyn Village Workshops, Cemmaes Road, Machynlleth, Montgomeryshire SY20 8LY

© Text: Geoff Elliott 2004
© Maps & illustrations: Morag Perrott 2004
First edition 2004

We would like to thank the Wales Tourist Board for allowing us to use the main cover photograph.

Cover pictures: *Main* – Harlech Castle © WTB 2004. *Inset* – Near Senigl, Walk 3. Geoff Elliott.

Printed on evolution recycled paper by: WPG, Welshpool, Powys.

ISBN: 1 902302 28 1